FAMILY LIFE

A SIMPLE GUIDE *to the* BIBLICAL FAMILY

FAMILY LIFE

A SIMPLE GUIDE to the BIBLICAL FAMILY

KEVIN SWANSON

Generations
PASSING ON THE FAITH

Published by:
Generations
19039 Plaza Dr. Ste. #210
Parker, Colorado, 80134

For more information on this and
other titles from Generations,
visit www.generations.org or call 1-888-389-9080.

CONTENTS

Preface.. 7

Introduction 9

1 The Christian Family.. 19

2 Family Relationships 43

3 Family Devotion... 66

4 Family Discipleship and Character Training 84

5 The Family Economy 109

6 Family Honor.. 125

7 Family Culture.. 138

8 Family Education 158

9 Family, Church, & State 176

Appendix – The Gen2 Survey 194

Notes.. 205

Scripture Index.. 210

PREFACE

Although I have spoken on family issues at hundreds of conferences over the last twenty years, I held off on writing a book on
the family until now. I am glad that I did. Life has a way of humbling
us. Pride and self-confidence are endemic among the younger sort.
As I put it to a couple of young men I was mentoring once: "When I
was your age, I was smarter than you. Now, I'm dumber." Experience
and trials, as interpreted by God's Word, yield wisdom. In the physical world of human experiences, you are not an expert in kayaking
the rapids until you have navigated a hundred rivers, ten times each.
Raising children is something like riding the rapids. Wisdom gained
from experience helps us to see what God meant when He revealed
the nuggets on family life in Scripture. It gives a context in which we
can understand and apply those truths. In the words of Jesus Christ,
the Wisdom of God, it is those who do the truth that come to the light
(John 3:21). This experiential wisdom is vital to understanding the
ditches that parents, myself included, can fall into on either side of
the road as they discern the perfect will of God.

For years I tried to avoid critiquing any particular child-raising expert or author—and there are thousands of them out there. Instead, I recommended to parents that they obtain five to six resources on the subject. I told them to digest the good stuff and spit out the bones. No single person can serve as the compendium of all knowledge in this area, except God. Moreover, a single expert cannot conceive of every possible situation that confronts every family in the world. "Where no counsel is, the people fall: but in the multitude of counselors there is safety" (Prov. 11:14). What more important thing will we do with our lives than raise our children? Therefore, I encourage every parent to rely on a multitude of counselors and authors concerning these matters.

I really wanted to write a little book on a big topic. The best books are usually short on content and long on wisdom that comes first from biblical principles. There are many books written on the different aspects of family life, but I wanted to write a short overview of a big topic stuffed with as much wisdom as I could assemble. When we think about theology, family life, or anything, we tend to lose the forest in the trees even more so than we would lose the trees in the bird's eye view of the forest. The trick is to see the forest and the trees without losing sight of one or the other. My hope is that this sweeping vision of the entire picture of the biblical family will make some contribution to this end.

INTRODUCTION

I n the 1890s, the "Farmer Boy" Almanzo Wilder and the "Prairie Girl" Laura Ingalls grew up in homes and families very different from the ones we find in our world today. We read their stories in the book series called *Little House on the Prairie*. In their world, there were no "Gay and Lesbian Education Networks"[1] in the one-room school-houses in New York State and South Dakota where they were raised. They didn't know about transgendered kids. They did not own iPods. They had no teen idols. They worked side by side with their parents every day, all through the year. Of course, there was no real problem with pornography addictions among the teenage boys. It certainly wasn't as high as 80%. There was no internet, no television, and no movie theaters. Mr. Anthony Comstock was prosecuting a few operations that were sending lewd pictures of immodestly-dressed women through the U.S. Postal Service. A few prostitutes in New York City might have attempted illegal abortions with Madame Restell, a nineteenth-century abortionist. There were no sexual education classes in the high schools, abstinence-only or otherwise. There were no Plan B pills for the sexually active 15-year-old girls. Abortifacients were only known in the dens of prostitutes in the large cities, and nobody thought of bringing up contraception in pre-marital counseling in the evangelical churches of the day. Almanzo and Laura had never met a teenage girl with anorexia. Not a single child in their neighborhood was placed on prescription psychotropic drugs. Illegitimacy existed in some of the larger cities, but it was almost unheard of in the small towns. They used another word for illegitimacy—"bastardy." Only 1% to 2% of children were born outside of wedlock, and divorces were similarly rare. Popular songs would not make even a single mention of the "F" word. Katy Perry was not encouraging fourteen-year-old girls to lesbianism. Eminem was not referring to his own mother as a female dog. In fact, the most popular song in the 1880s, "My Grandfather's Clock," offered honor to a grandfather for the life he lived from his birth to his death.

Some folks would probably laugh at a world like that, but others cannot bring themselves to laugh because they are in shock. As the stark contrast between old and new comes into view, they can briefly make out the tragic devastation in modern family culture. They see that the family is badly broken. Though our civilization is still propped up by our wealth, psychotropic drugs, social welfare programs, and expensive education systems, it is all a house of cards. There is an appearance of functionality, but it is a cheap facade. A society with a 60% to 70% illegitimacy rate will never survive in the long run.

The disintegration of the family unit affects the nice, middle-income Christian family almost as much as the rest of the population. Illegitimate divorce and remarriage rates are much higher in the Christian Church now than they were in 1910, by orders of magnitude. Relationships are tenuous. Based on statistics easily accessible from Internet service providers, the highest pornography download

rates are found in states and counties with the highest church attendance rates.[2] Christian churches and families are afflicted with pornography addiction at higher rates than the rest of the population,
according to CovenantEyes.com.[3] About 80% of young men visit pornography websites on a weekly or monthly basis. These sorts of statistics point to symptoms of very deep problems in our society. Certainly, this news should cause tremendous grief and alarm among
Christians, though the rest of the world will likely accept them as
the inevitable realities of modern life. Still others are encouraged to
persist in their own sinful conditions when they realize many others
are likewise afflicted.

Emancipation for young women from the home is by far the norm,
and any young woman who maintains anything of a family-orient-
ed mindset from 18 to 30 years of age is the exception to the rule.
Contraceptive use among evangelicals is higher than ever, despite
the constant warnings concerning the abortifacient effects upon the
lives of many little ones. Increasingly, Christian pastors and theologians are seeing connections between the rise in homosexuality
and the use of contraceptives and pornography. Hedonism and the
idolizing of pleasure trumps God's creation mandates in the minds
of many professing Christians in the West. Feminism, as defined by
Betty Freidan and Gloria Steinem, is almost universally received by
Christians from all denominations. Family economies, as defined
and assumed by passages like Proverbs 31:11 and 1 Timothy 5:14,
hardly exist anymore in the mind of the evangelical family. Male
headship is a term barely mentioned in whispers here and there in
the Church. The male is hardly considered responsible for the material sustenance of the home anymore (1 Tim. 5:8), and the Christian
Church hesitates to address the problem of male abdication. Something is rotting in Western society, and Christians seem reticent to
"come out from among them," as the Lord told us to do.

As the family disintegrates, the world counters by offering state-trained professionals to raise children: they provide free education, daycare, and food for hundreds of millions of children in Western nations. These are not state-funded boarding schools or orphanages. However, they do serve as part-time surrogate parents, like those first configured by Jean-Jacques Rousseau, who masterminded the modern state while leaving five of his children on the steps of an orphanage as soon as they were born.[4] He then proceeded to write books on modern education, encouraging state intervention into the nurture of the child. Generation after generation, state institutions have been growing stronger while family relationships have been weakening.

The world scoffs at the Christian ethos and ethic, but it is hard to pay attention to somebody who laughs hysterically in the face of his own execution, as the trap door of the gallows releases under his feet. The mainstream media, the universities, and the world's trained psychologists have nothing for which to commend themselves. They have proven their utter failure beyond a doubt over the last hundred years. They have experimented with an entire social system, and the results have been found wanting. The experiment is over, and the fruit of their labors is manifest: the disintegration of the family and human society as we used to know it.

The Tragic Breakdown of Fatherhood

During the previous ten generations, from 1800 to 1960, the family economy collapsed and fatherhood disintegrated. Following the weakening of fatherhood came the breakdown of the family in tandem with the sexual revolution of the 1960s. The most pronounced and irrefutable attestation to the fact of social disintegration and the breakdown of the family came with the rise of homosexuality in the entire Western world. When the United States Supreme Court provided the highest approval and official certification of the homosexual lifestyle in 2015 (with the Obergefell V. Hodges ruling), it sealed the fate of an entire civilization. Social systems had eroded gradually over the previous hundred years, and the Supreme Court of the United States only placed a headstone on the grave.

Christian leaders have struggled to assign causes for the revolutionary breakdown seen in human society. In the book of Romans, the Apostle Paul traces this sexual nihilism to God's judgment and a depraved mind (Rom. 1:26-28). As the state of the family collapsed at the turn of the 20th Century, a well-known family leader attempted an explanation for the conditions that prepared the world for the wholesale acceptance of homosexuality. Dr. James Dobson pointed out that a major "nurture" influence upon a young man yielding homosexual inclinations is the "lack of a loving, respectful relationship with a father."[5] Of course, every young man born and/or raised without a father does not turn into a homosexual. There are other factors involved, but fatherhood is basic. The illegitimacy problem we face today is fatherlessness at a fundamental level. With the millennial generation, 57% of little boys are born without a father.[6] That's a nine-fold increase over the illegitimacy rate recorded in the early 1960s, when only six percent of little boys were born without fathers. It was this generation born in the 1960s that contributed to the total social and political acceptance of homosexuality in the 2000s, and the complete reversal of public policy relating to the family. If that is the case, what can we expect for the future? Given that the problem of illegitimacy and the general disintegration of the family is nine times worse today than it was in 1960, what will the devastation look like in the year 2050? It is hard to imagine. We have yet to completely understand all of the pathologies, social effects, spiritual effects, and economic effects that will result from the wholesale fatherlessness of the 1990s, 2000s, and 2010s.

One thing we do know: a father is important to the life of every little boy. To afflict a fatherless child and to purposely create fatherless children, is a shameful, oppressive, and wicked thing (Ex. 22:22-24).

We Are Broken

"So what's the big deal?" the modern mind asks. "We have never had so much wealth and scientific technology. We have never been so proud and so strong. Ever. 'We are rich, and increased with goods, and we have need of nothing'" (Rev. 3:17). What the modern nations do not realize is that they are wretched, miserable, poor, blind, and naked.

If, by the grace of God, we have seen our true condition, our first response is brokenness. We begin with poverty of spirit (Matt. 5:3). We offer first a sacrifice of a broken and a contrite heart (Ps. 51:17). It is the pattern of the Publican who falls down on his face and cries out, God have mercy on me a sinner!" (Luke 18:13). All self-justifications, blame-shifting, minimization of the problem, and arguments for tolerance are set aside. There is no more resistance against those who point out the problems, no more accusations of "judgmentalism." There is only the humble and the contrite heart, and the spirit broken into a hundred pieces. The lack of brokenness is the major problem with liberalism, evangelicalism, and fundamentalism in this country. The nation is self-contented and self-reliant. There is very little broken spirit in our family books today, and for that reason there isn't much hope for revival. Wherever there is true humility and brokenness before God, there will be restoration, forgiveness, and redemption in His Son, Jesus Christ.

Because of the remnants of the fall, we all start out broken, and there is nowhere that this so clearly reveals itself as in family life. Both functional families and dysfunctional families need grace. For those who are not broken, we truly have nothing that we can say to them. This book is not for them. It doesn't matter whether this is the proud homosexual family (who is very happy with their dysfunctionality), or the proud Christian homeschooling family (who is very happy with their "functionality"). Only those who are on their faces crying out, "God have mercy on me, a sinner!" will find the grace to live this life (Luke 18:13).

The last forty years of Christian teaching on family have produced "recipe" oriented methods of child raising. When I have been called to teach on raising children, I have presented one simple recipe. It goes like this:

Step 1. Get down on your face before God.
Step 2. Cry out in true sincerity, "God have mercy! Oh God, have mercy! Please have mercy on me and my poor family!"

Formulaic methods for raising a godly family give the mistaken impression that we are capable for these things. When it came to his own ministry, the Apostle Paul cried out, "Who is sufficient for these things?" (2 Cor. 2:16). Every Christian parent with a proper conception of human nature and the challenges before him will say the same thing. We must not present the Christian life or the Christian family as somehow manageable outside of relying on the grace of God. We are both justified by grace and sanctified by grace — it is all of grace. "By grace ye are saved through faith, and that not of yourselves it is the gift of God" (Eph. 2:8-9). As God works in us to will and to do of His good pleasure (Phil. 2:11-12), we are expected to work out our salvation (in this sanctification process). We will therefore seek to apply God's principles in reliance on the grace of God. But reducing the process to a man-made set of rules always ends in faithlessness and self-reliance.

We Are Redeemed

The Christian father and mother begin the journey of raising their children on their knees. They cry out with the Philippian jailor, "What must I do to be saved?" Then, like him, they believe on the Lord Jesus Christ, and their entire household is baptized (Acts 16:31-34). Their brokenness is never entirely forgotten, but the new man in Christ begins to manifest himself. This is the beginning of a journey like that of Christiana and her children in the second book of John Bunyan's *Pilgrim's Progress*, who all set out on the pilgrim pathway together, assuming household unity. The regenerating influence of the Holy Spirit upon a father or mother produces an entirely different kind of family. It is what we call a "covenantal family."

The Christian parents saved by the redemptive work of the Son of God, now raise their children "in the Lord." This is a strange phrase, not used very much by modern Christians. However, I want to use biblical language when describing children who are raised in a Christian home. The atmosphere, the attitudes, the priorities, and the methods are very different in a Christian home than in a non-Christian home. The fundamental reason for this is that Christian parents are in relationship with Jesus Christ, who is their Teacher, Savior, and Lord. They live in the grace of Christ. They operate in the love of God. They are constantly aware of the forgiveness of God. They have a new identity as servants of Christ, and sons of the heavenly Father.

Family by Faith

The just will live by faith, and he will lead his family by faith. "But without faith it is impossible to please Him: for he that comes to God must believe that He is, and that He is a rewarder of them that diligently seek Him" (Heb. 11:6).

Another reason why formulaic family life is counter-biblical is that it doesn't take much faith to paint by numbers. When you are painting by numbers, somebody tells you what to color yellow and what to color blue. On the other hand, it takes faith to sculpt something out of a piece of rock. Raising children is more like sculpting. Every family's situation is unique in that God brings differing trials along and each must be addressed with faith and prayerfulness. It is God's purpose and delight that we act in faith, and not out of fear of man or self-reliance.

When I left my position in corporate management with all of the attendant securities in exchange for a little more time to disciple my family and start our family ministry, we braced ourselves for the big pay cut. It was a step of faith for my wife and me, but we watched God provide for us in amazing ways. Every time we have acted in faith, we have seen God's hand more evident in our lives and the blessings flow. In an honest moment, most parents would tell you that they feel inadequate to the task of raising their kids. They may think it easier at points to hand them over to professionals. When you bring your kids home and you get into their lives and they get into yours, you will soon discover the task to be impossible, short of the grace of God. This is especially true for those who are concerned about the spiritual well-being of their children. A CEO of a Fortune 500 company may be able to handle his staff with the techniques he has picked up in his organizational behavior classes at Harvard; but when he comes home in the evening, a strong-willed two-year-old will bring that man to his knees as he realizes what he is up against.

Every family crisis serves as a test of faith. The Bible gives us the example of the ultimate family crisis when Job lost every one of his children and all of his household possessions in a single day. It was one of the largest tests of faith of all time. In his grief and agony, and despite his wife encouraging him to curse God, Job would not waver in his faith. In what some may take as outrageous hyperbole, Job confessed to God, "Though He slay me, yet will I trust in Him" (Job 13:15). Job was determined to hold on to the fact that God knew what He was doing in this crisis. He was fully convinced that God was behind his afflictions, when he proclaimed, "The Lord gives, and the Lord takes away. Blessed be the Name of the Lord!" It is one thing to give tacit assent to God's sovereignty. It is quite another thing to be able to say it in the cauldron of affliction, as with Christ in the garden, "Not My will, but Thine be done."

For most of us, our spouses and children are our dearest possessions on earth. Thus, family crises form a real test of our commitment to God, our love for God, and our trust in God. When worshiping and serving God takes second priority to our family, that is idolatry. When fathers and mothers give way to idolatry of any kind, their children usually follow suit with their own choices of idols. This is a very common pattern for "Christian" families today. Children get the message loud and clear as they watch their parents prioritize their family relationships over their relationship with God. Our love for our children must be a derivative of our love for God. The first and greatest commandment must never be compromised in the accomplishment of the second. We love the Lord our God with heart, soul, mind, and strength, *and then* we love our neighbor as ourselves (Matt. 22:38). Should we attempt the second without the first, we are giving way to idolatry and we will fail to really love others.

Family relationships and family life form the anvil on which God applies His hammer to us. He forms us more and more into the image of Christ using trial, suffering, and loss. By faith, we see His hand working on us and we are thankful. We must believe that He has a good end in mind (Rom. 8:28), and we continue to hope in His mercy, year after year.

1 THE CHRISTIAN FAMILY

Ten years ago, our radio ministry assembled a series of interviews called "Will the Circle Be Unbroken?" It was based on the old Gospel song written in 1907 that contemplated a family reunion in heaven:

I was standing by my window
On one cold and cloudy day
When I saw that hearse come rolling
For to carry my mother away

Will the circle be unbroken
By and by, Lord, by and by
There's a better home a-waiting
In the sky, Lord, in the sky.

These words very much express the heart of every godly parent. We desire generational continuity in the faith. There is no greater joy than to hear that our children are walking in the truth! Every time we read 3 John 4 as Christian parents, we want to say "Amen!" So, for these interviews, I sought out ordinary Christian fathers who had raised families in the 1970s and whose children were all walking with the Lord three decades later.

When I asked my own father to share some of his thoughts on this series of programs, his response surprised me. He suggested that I interview one of the leaders of the large Christian family ministries. Unwittingly, it seems, my father shared with me the "secret" of success for a Christian family—humility. He really felt that others had more important things to say about parenting and family life than he did. Looking back, I can see that I was raised in a rather obscure, unpretentious, pious, and humble family. I recall my early years with fondness, largely for this reason. Of course, my parents were not perfect, but I consider it nothing short of the grace of God that I was so privileged to be raised by Ralph and Carol Swanson in the 1960s and 1970s. I know that they still pray for their children and grandchildren every day, and I can tell you that God has answered those prayers.

Consider all that stands against us, as we attempt to build our families. We are all born with a sin problem that affects each of our children. There is no parent without sin; Christian parents included. The things that destroy the family are more prevalent in society today than they were 200 years ago. The entire spirit of the age blows like a hurricane against family integration, family relationships, and family solidarity. Now more than ever, no family will make it short of the grace of God.

We cannot make it without the wisdom of the Word of God. Too many books on child raising and family life rely upon psychological studies, bad theology, personal experience, helpful suggestions, and the like. When parents have relied too heavily on these books, many have seen terrible results, even a generational wandering from the Christian faith. It is possible to lead your family badly. If a father fell asleep at the wheel or made some other poor choice while driving his family down a highway, the results could be catastrophic. It is definitely possible to blow it, and many have. There are many ways to go wrong. Ignoring God's wisdom in His Word or displacing it with human wisdom is the first mistake. For these important reasons, we want to stick very close to biblical language and biblical principle as we describe the biblical family.

The Biblical Household

The Bible affirms the household, or the family, as the basic social unit. Marriage is highly encouraged, and warnings are issued for those who unwisely delay it.

> "But if they cannot exercise self-control, let them marry. For it is better to marry than to burn with passion." (1 Cor. 7:9)

> "Therefore I desire that the younger widows marry, bear children, manage the house, give no opportunity to the adversary to speak reproachfully. For some have already turned aside after Satan." (1 Tim. 5:14-15)

The above passages clearly frown on the undue delay of marriage, which is important for the millennial generation to note. There are ditches on both sides of this road. An over-emphasis on singleness can become a doctrine of demons (1 Tim. 4:1-3), according to the same Apostle who recommended singleness during times of crisis.

> "Now concerning virgins: I have no commandment from the Lord; yet I give judgment as one whom the Lord in His mercy has made trustworthy. I suppose therefore that this is good because of the present distress—that it is good for a man to remain as he is." (1 Cor. 7:25-26)

Somehow, in the history of the Church somebody missed the phrase "the present distress," and the doctrine of demons emerged over the centuries. However, from creation onward, God instituted marriage as the way that humans should live their lives. Jesus Christ noted exceptions to the rule in three cases: those born eunuchs, those who are forcibly made eunuchs (usually by tyrannical governments), and those who make themselves eunuchs for the kingdom of God (Matt. 19:10-12). Then He added, "He who is able to accept it, let him accept it."

Here, Jesus does not refer to the modern metrosexual who delays marriage and glorifies singleness and perpetual adolescent immaturity. Of course, this lifestyle must include free indulgence in pornography and fornication. Meanwhile, Christian kids grow up in this same social system of extended adolescence in their schools and church groups, while desperately trying to avoid as much fornication as possible. Pornography addictions for young men exceed 80%, and the problem is often worse for professing Christians. Dragging pornography addictions into marriage has proven disastrous, so these Christian young men are even less prepared for marriage than ever before. According to the National Campaign to Prevent Teen and Unplanned Pregnancy, 80% of evangelical unmarried persons confess to having committed fornication, compared to 88% of the rest of the population.[7]

When a secular writer from CNN grappled with these statistics, he ended the article with the question, "So what should a Christian parent or youth pastor do? How do they convince more young Christians to wait until marriage, or should they stop even trying?"[8] The Christian "True Love Waits" campaigns have proven themselves unable to stand against the social systems into which these young people are tossed. Unless we recover a full-orbed discipleship approach for our youth that prepares them for work and marriage, our Christian youth will hardly be salvaged from this bleak milieu.

The answer that few people today really want to accept is that found in 1 Corinthians 7:9 and 1 Timothy 5:14-15 (above). Somehow, it is considered odd and even immoral for a 16, 17, or 18-year-old man or woman to desire marriage. The alternative offered by the world is fifteen years of serial fornicating relationships, but real Christians and practical Christians would find this completely unacceptable. We prefer the wisdom of Scripture to the wisdom of this world. "It is better to marry than to burn with passion" (1 Cor. 7:9).

Granted, each man and woman has individual gifting and a unique calling and nobody is recommending a one-size-fits-all approach to marriage and singleness. Nevertheless, the spite for marriage and family has done immeasurable damage to the Christian Church in the West.

Our Lord Jesus affirmed the creation mandate in his teaching when He said, "Have you not read that He who made them at the beginning 'made them male and female,' and said, 'For this reason a man shall leave his father and mother and be joined to his wife, and the two shall become one flesh'? So then, they are no longer two but one flesh. Therefore, what God has joined together, let not man separate" (Matt. 19:4b-6).

The single life apart from the covenant family and church is more the way of Cain (who wandered as a vagabond east of Eden) than the way of Christ. Notice that I include the covenant church family as a place where the celibate may still find his or her identity. What we do not read here in the words of the Lord is, "Therefore a man shall leave his father and mother, and be joined to his college apartment and the single life until he is 35 years old at which point he may or may not be joined to his wife." The world's social conditioning weans our young singles from the family ethos. Occasionally, we caution our young people about the alternate worldviews they will encounter at secular and Christian college campuses, but they should be equally aware of the alternate *social views* as well.

The Biblical household then is formed when a young man leaves his parents' household and cleaves to his wife, and they form another household. As the young man lived in day-to-day covenant family relationship before marriage, the hope is that he was growing in selflessness and the fruits of the spirit in relationship to those with whom he lived. The life of the vagabond configured by the modern social system, apart from covenant family and church is rooted in an existentialism in which self becomes preeminent.

Marriage

"They are no longer two but one flesh."

Here we discover a "great mystery" (Eph. 5:32). Christian theology and sociology involves mystery, and if you are a Christian you need to get used to operating within the realm of mystery. Failure to handle this mystery rightly has led to a wrong view of the family and the Church over the centuries, particularly in America where individualism is king. The superficial view sees the two people as separate only because the two are separated by spatial distance. The text does not indicate that the two are one in spirit, but one in flesh, and flesh is understood materially. The oneness is more ultimate than the individual two-ness.

Those pastors and Christian authors who have a hard time seeing the oneness of marriage will use words like "leader" to describe the husband's role. The Bible does not use this word because the Scriptures think covenantally. Instead, the word preferred by the inspired writers is "head."

"For the husband is head of the wife, as also Christ is head of the church; and He is the Savior of the body." (Eph. 5:23)

Be careful with doctrinal teachings that treat the husband as merely a "leader." To be the head of a body is much different from being a manager of a company or a leader of a military troop. The difference is seen in the covenantal nature of the family and church that God has hard-wired into these institutions. The difference between a leader and a head of a body is seen in the organic connection. A leader is not organically connected to his troops as "one flesh," as is Christ with His Church and the husband with his wife.

Modern individualism has led to both feminism and a warped view of male leadership and pagan patriarchalism. With feminism, the woman pulls away from the oneness by competing for "leadership" in the home. Competition should be completely irrelevant in true oneness. How does the torso of a body compete with the head? The pagan patriarchalist likewise ignores this oneness, failing to recognize the woman as bone of his bone and flesh of his flesh. He sees no complementation, only competition and something else to subjugate.

A clearer understanding of this headship will lead to many profound implications for the family. For example, the head will be less likely to beat on his own body, as a leader might with the troops. Moreover, the head will take responsibility for the body, while looking out for the body's best interest. The head will claim the body's problems for his own, and be willing to sacrifice for it. The body finds it impossible to be the head, and the head finds it impossible to take the place of the body. When one or the other ceases to function, the entire unit becomes incapacitated. They both serve in complementary roles, and neither can deprecate the other without sustaining damage to itself.

This unity is something that really does exist, and it is a unity that must be increasingly realized, cultivated, and acted upon. The unity is an ontological fact, whether people recognize it or not. Recognizing and appreciating the unity will better sustain and nurture it. Failing to recognize and nurture the unity will often yield disastrous consequences. Covenantal thinking in marriage is crucial. Before a couple gets married, I tell them that they are about to recite 120 words that will change their lives in the most profound way. These words form a superglue that attaches two pieces of cardboard, and this connection cannot be undone. By God's ordination, the two will become one, and to change their minds after the vows are made is as fruitless as separating the two pieces of cardboard once the glue has set.

This marital oneness should be cultivated through communication, intimacy, economics, ministry, Bible study, and worship. While the unity can be compromised and destroyed by neglect and infidelity, the Christian couple can also nurture that unity on a daily basis. This is how we form the rebar in the foundation of the family.

The Roles of Husband and Wife

The Scripture gives clear and distinct roles for the husband and the wife, and these should be taken into careful consideration by every family. Given that our sons and daughters will probably marry, we ought to take into consideration their future roles as husbands and wives as we prepare them for adult life. In a few cases, we will know for certain that a child will not marry. In other cases, we may be uncertain. However, most of the time we can count on our children moving towards marriage and fulfilling the creation ordinance. Thus, these roles should play heavily upon parents as they think about preparing their children for the calling God has upon their lives.

Role differences make for one of the most (if not the most) controversial subjects of our day. Entire social systems were designed to eliminate all role differences, and it is the highest heresy to question these systems. The root doctrine that the modern egalitarians find so reprehensible is the notion that men differ from women or that men were created differently than women, with a different physical and emotional make-up. The fact that men have no wombs in which to provide gestation for a child is of constant irritation to the role egalitarians. They argue with God, and they have attempted to reinvent gender on a wholesale level. In consequence, they have ruined entire civilizations with their new social theories. Christians, however, should ignore the foolishness of modern social scientists and return to what God said about roles.

1. The husband is responsible for the material well-being of the family (1 Tim. 5:8).
2. The husband is to be the "resident theologian" in the home and be able to answer questions his wife may have concerning what they have learned in the church (1 Cor. 14:34-35).
3. The husband is primarily responsible for bringing the children up in the nurture of the Lord (Eph. 6:4, Deut. 6:7).
4. The husband is to love his wife sacrificially, as Christ loved the Church and gave Himself for her (Eph. 5:25).
5. The husband is to live with his wife in an understanding way and treat her with gentleness and respect (1 Pet. 3:7).
6. The husband is responsible for providing the conjugal needs of his wife (1 Cor. 7:3).
7. The husband is responsible for taking dominion over God's creation, with his wife as his help made appropriate for him in the task (Gen. 1:28, Gen. 2:18-22).
8. The husband is responsible for defending his wife, sons, and daughters from deadly force (Neh. 4:14).

The wife's responsibilities are also laid out clearly
in biblical passages:

1. The wife is the help appropriate for her husband in his dominion tasks (Gen. 2:20b-22).
2. The wife is the home manager or home administrator
   (1 Tim. 5:14, Prov. 31:27).
3. The wife is called to be a "homemaker" (Tit. 2:5).
4. The wife is called to submit to her husband in the Lord
   (Eph. 5:22, 33).
5. The wife is called to love her husband and her children
   (Tit. 2:4).
6. The wife is called to seek the betterment of the household
   economy (Prov. 31:11-27).
7. The wife is responsible for providing the conjugal needs of
   her husband (1 Cor. 7:3).

Whenever God through His Word directs a certain injunction towards an elder, a civil leader, an employee, an employer, a husband,
or a wife, He defines a special role and a particular responsibility.
It should be assumed that what is required of the employer is not
equally expected of the employee. What is required of the civil mag-
istrate in Romans 13:4b (to be "an avenger to execute wrath on him
who practices evil") is not equally expected of the rest of us as established by Romans 12:19b ("do not avenge yourselves.") This does
not preclude other injunctions or responsibilities, but it does enjoin
a particular emphasis. Wives are to submit to their husbands and
husbands are to love their wives. Of course, there are points at which
the husband should submit to the wisdom provided by his wife, and
the wife ought also to love her husband in sacrificial ways. Mainly and finally, the wife should submit to her husband's directions
and obey him (even if she should disagree with him). Only in cases

when his directions constitute a clear and obvious conflict with the laws of God should she consider disobeying. Then, I would recommend her doing this only after consultation with the elders in her church assembly.

The Christian family must remember that all of this takes place "in the Lord." Children obey "in the Lord," wives submit "in the Lord," and husbands love their wives "in the Lord" (Col. 3:18, Eph. 6:1). Doing something "in the Lord" assumes that we are in relationship with Christ as we perform these duties. To take on these roles apart from our relationship in Christ is too heavy of a burden for anybody. A wife who realizes the Son of God Himself washed her feet (and her heart), with his own blood, will find that it is not a heavy burden to submit to her own husband in the Lord. In our union with Christ we abide in the love of God. If His love is shed abroad in the heart of the husband, he will live out the same sacrificial love towards his wife.

In the Christian home, Christ must become the overriding reality of our entire life and existence. When the Apostle Paul begins the practical section of his epistle to the Ephesians, he mentions the Lord Jesus Christ nine times in the eleven verses dealing with marriage (Eph. 5:22-33). He can barely speak ten words before he mentions Christ again. This typifies for us one who lives in relationship with Christ. While the quantity of "Christ-mentions" is not the essential issue, the presence of the Christ-consciousness is of essence. Occasionally, we should think to ask the question: "When was the last time Jesus was mentioned in this home? Ask yourself, "Am I reading books that deal with practical issues on family and marriage, but seeming to drift far from the atoning work of Christ, His love for us, and His lordship over us?" If you read through the practical books relating to the family and find zero references to Christ in the first one hundred pages, at the very least you may conclude it was not written by the Apostle Paul.

When we live in relationship with Christ, we experience the fellowship of His sufferings. We suffer as He suffered. We love the unlovable. We hug the un-huggable. We forgive the unforgivable. We begin to see others as Christ sees them. We interact with them as He would. We submit to others because we submit to the will of the Father, as He did.

The marriage will always be tested during seasons of trial. It is most difficult for a wife to honor her husband when he is acting dishonorably—angry, controlling, uncommunicative, passive, and unwilling to lead. It is most difficult for the husband to love his wife when she is most unlovable—emotionally unstable, nagging, accusatory, angry, and bitter. These are times of testing. When the husband loves his wife despite all of that, and when the wife submits to her husband despite all of that, the Christian marriage will find Christ's redemption working in a truly marvelous way.

A Christian couple must never find themselves in a Mexican standoff—a confrontation in which "no participant can proceed or retreat without being exposed to danger." When a wife insists that she will not submit until her husband begins to love her as Christ loved the Church, and the husband insists he will not love his wife until she begins to submit to him, we have a Mexican standoff. Neither wish to expose themselves to danger, but that is exactly what Christ calls them to do. We must be willing to suffer with Him as He suffered. This is precisely the message of Ephesians 5:22-33 and 1 Peter 2:15-3:4. Couples who are hamstrung in this horrible condition are not walking with Christ.

Several months ago, I asked my children what they could recall about our marriage. They have lived with us continually over the last twenty years, and I was surprised by their response. They couldn't think of any conflicts, difficulties, or dysfunctional conditions. Of course, if we had replayed videos that recorded our marriage every day for twenty-five years, this would not have been the assessment. In the end though, it is love and forgiveness that washes away all the hurtful words, the bitterness, the hard-heartedness, the grumpiness, the nagging, the blaming, and the anger that appeared here and there throughout the years. This manifests the power of love. The love of Christ and forgiveness is what remains in the minds of ourselves and our children, even though our home really did contain a great deal of sin through the years.

The Biblical Purpose of Marriage and Family

God's purpose for the family is clearly laid out in Scripture, and must be realized by every Christian family on an everyday basis. At the creation of the man and the woman, notice the dominion mandate God gave to them.

> "So God created man in His own image; in the image of God He created him; male and female He created them. Then God blessed them, and God said to them, 'Be fruitful and multiply; fill the earth and subdue it; have dominion over the fish of the sea, over the birds of the air, and over every living thing that moves on the earth.'" (Gen. 1:27-28)

Purpose #1. Child Bearing

The first purpose for marriage is to be fruitful and to multiply. This was confirmed again by God's directive to Noah after the flood (Gen. 9:1).

The 2015 Supreme Court ruling on the Obergefell case marked the final cultural break from every vestige of a Christian heritage; and it did something else. This action taken by the most powerful human court in the world redefined the human family for the first time since God ordained the family at creation. It is a brave new world indeed.

At root is that the hearts of men are in rebellion against God's law order for the family. Also, modern man has increasingly rejected

God's order of procreation and dominion. God demands procreation at the same time that He provides pleasure within the context of marriage. Since 1960, modern man has discovered more convenient ways to separate sexuality from procreation employing pornography and self-fulfillment, homosexuality, and birth control.

After Obergefell, leading evangelical voices are connecting the dots between the legalization of homosexual marriage and contraception (think of it as sex without babies). Albert Mohler, the president of the largest Baptist seminary in the world, made this connection in his recent book *We Cannot Be Silent.*

> We are clearly at a very important turning point, but you have to go back to the early 20th century when sexual revolutionaries largely funded an effort to separate sex and procreation, and that was birth control. And most Christians seem to think today that birth control was just something that came along as something of a scientific or medical development. They fail to see that it was driven by moral revolutionaries who knew that you couldn't have a moral revolution, you especially couldn't have a sexual revolution, unless you could separate sex and babies.[9]

Pastor John MacArthur drew a similar conclusion in a message given on July 19, 2015 after the infamous Supreme Court decision. In his words,

> If you go back to contraception, you go back to where this all began. It is the product, admittedly, of the feminist movement. Go back through contraception; now when contraception comes in, you have sex without children.[10]

As contraception attempted to separate sexual pleasure and personal convenience from procreation, modern society was forced to accept abortion and abortifacients as part of the equation. At least eighty million babies turned into collateral damage in this great so-cio-sexual revolution (here in this country).

It was Planned Parenthood's founder, Margaret Sanger who obtained funding for the development of the birth control pill in the 1950s. No other individual has contributed to more killings of human beings than this woman. Over half the world's population has been killed by abortion or abortifacients (or prevented by contraception) since 1960.[11] While abortion rates in this country have fallen since 1990, the use of abortifacients like Plan B pills and IUD's have increased 500% over the last 12 years. Surprisingly, Evangelicals use these highly effective forms of birth control at higher rates than Catholics and mainline Protestants. These highly effective forms prevent implantation of the baby in the uterus, and thereby create hazardous conditions that contribute to the death of the child.

Use of Highly Effective Forms of Birth Control (by Religion)[12]

Catholic Women - 68%
Mainline Protestants - 73%
Evangelicals - 74%

God's Word imposes criminal penalties on those who create hazardous conditions in which a child might lose his life (Ex. 21:22-25). While almost every country in the world has legalized abortion, and have enthusiastically embraced the use of abortifacients, Christians need to take the opposite stand. To purposefully kill a child in its mother's womb ought to be a crime. Certainly, it is a sin. Also, to purposefully create hazardous conditions in the womb for the unborn child (by taking a drug that would thin the endometrium of the uterine wall) is a violation of the sixth commandment (Ex. 20:13).

For many years, evangelical leaders were either silent on the use of contraceptives, or they actually encouraged their use. The few that spoke against it were ignored or mocked. However, things are finally changing. As Albert Mohler insisted in his book published in 2016, "We must not be silent."[13]

It is when sexual pleasure trumps procreation, discipleship, and kingdom work that we fail to realize the purpose of God in marriage and life (Matt. 6:33). Too many modern church-goers are taken by the idolatry of sensuality, whether it be physical intimacy, food, drink, or entertainment. With all their hearts, they seek a life of material well-being, personal peace and affluence, and physical pleasure. This, of course, is the wrong god. When these things become more important than the worship of God, the service of Christ, the kingdom of God and His righteousness, then it is plain that this is no Christian family.

Are there reasons for holding back on having children? Health problems? Money issues? Spiritual struggles in the home? The Bible does explicitly allow for birth control in certain situations.

"Do not deprive one another except with consent for a time, that you may give yourselves to fasting and prayer." (1 Cor. 7:5).

Obviously, God allows an exception to regular sexual intimacy — prayer and fasting. Families go through times of physical and emotional crises, which cannot be separated from spiritual struggles. Moms have a hard time managing the household and the children. There may be physical problems that provide barriers to sexual intimacy or childbearing. These are reasons why a couple may choose to devote themselves to prayer and fasting.

Where a focus on pleasure trumps an interest in children, biblical dominion, and kingdom discipleship, not to mention prayer and fasting, it would seem that the mind is thinking more in a carnal manner than in a spiritual way. Pleasure is provided as a good gift from God to which we respond in gratefulness. However, the experience of physical pleasure can become self-oriented and take priority over the kingdom of God and His righteousness. We ought to be especially careful of these tendencies in a hedonistic age. The caution applies to couples in the child-bearing years and those beyond it.

Now, some may ask about the use of non-abortifacient birth control methods. For those considering these other methods, I have some questions to think about.

- Are you making this decision out of fear for the future, or faith? (Rom. 14:23)
- Have you taken into account the advice from 2,000 years of Church fathers who have taught on the issue (prior to the anti-family age we live in today)?[14]
- Is your life's purpose to give up your life for the Lord Jesus Christ, and not to save your life? Is this decision all part of giving up your life and taking up your cross and following the suffering Savior? (Matt. 10:39)
- Have you in any way given way to the materialism of the day, the self-centeredness bug, or the idolatry of sensuality?
- Have you done any prayer and fasting over this in the last month or two? Are you truly seeking God's will in this?
- Do you consider children a blessing, the fruit of the womb as His reward? At what point would you say that children are no longer a blessing? Can you defend that from Scripture?
- Are there any sins in your life that may need to be confessed, as James 5:16 encourages?
- Husband, if your wife was too weak and sickly to have sexual intimacy, would you be willing to embrace celibacy for months or years while you cared for her? Would you be willing to give your life for her?

Too often, secularism defines our values instead of God's Word. "Children are too expensive," they say.[15] Secular society will loudly commend the church community that has embraced debt for its "visionary programs," or where the birth rate is 0.8, or where women are forced to teach in the church for lack of men, and where young boys are more and more turning into homosexuals. This, they say is a very blessed community. Their values are very different from what Scripture presents. They have invented their own definition of good and evil. God's definitions of good and evil are very different. What we find in Deuteronomy 28:18, 44, Psalm 127, Romans 1:24, and Isaiah 3:12 clearly contradicts the secular vision for the community. Where the secular vision has been achieved by some community (as outlined above), we can conclude that this community must be under the curse of God. Clearly, passages like Psalm 127 define children as a blessing or a reward from the Lord.

> "Behold, children are a heritage from the Lord, the fruit of the womb is a reward. Like arrows in the hand of a warrior, so are the children of one's youth. Happy is the man who has his quiver full of them; they shall not be ashamed, but shall speak with their enemies in the gate." (Ps. 127:3-5)

This is hardly the perspective of the modern world, especially when a Christian family blessed with three or more children are constantly recipients of taunts and condemnation from the world. Any couple who has exceeded the 1.8 birth rate, will probably hear the question, "Are all those yours?" My wife responded to a grocery clerk who posed the question, saying "Yes! Five blessings. The woman replied, "I've got two. You want 'em?" Heart breaking, but that is the perspective shared by many who have learned the primacy of self and have not yet learned of the love of Jesus.

In His providence, God blesses certain families with more children than others. He blesses us in different ways. We should mostly be looking for His spiritual blessings, as in, the salvation of our households. So, we never look down upon any family who has not been similarly blessed in the ways in which we have been blessed. We rejoice with those who rejoice, and bless those who have been blessed. There is no place for envy, jealousy, and discontentment among the church of Jesus Christ.

Purpose #2 - Godly Offspring

For the covenant Christian family, the Lord provides another clearly stated purpose in Scripture, beyond that of merely populating the earth. He wants us populating heaven.

> "But did He not make them one, having a remnant of the Spirit? And why one? He seeks godly offspring. Therefore take heed to your spirit, and let none deal treacherously with the wife of his youth." (Mal. 2:15)

God seeks godly offspring in our Christian families. Does that surprise you? Here we find the vital importance of spiritual reproduction. It is more than physical reproduction, as emphasized in the creation ordinance and the Noahic covenant. Now, what the Lord expects from a Christian family is godly offspring. There is both a position of privilege and a responsibility to be found with these children. On the one hand, children born to one or more Christian parents are called "holy" (1 Cor. 7:14) by virtue of the fact they are born into the Christian family. Yet, these parents still have a responsibility to "bring them up in the nurture and the admonition of the Lord" (Eph. 6:4). Thus, merely birthing children into a Christian family doesn't "guarantee" godly seed, and neither does the nurture of a Christian family. Nevertheless, this is God's calling on the Christian family. The purpose for the Christian marriage is to have children and to disciple them into the kingdom of Jesus Christ. And, divorce is counter-productive to this end, according to Malachi 2:15.

> "But did He not make them one, having a remnant of the
> Spirit? And why one? He seeks godly offspring. Therefore
> take heed to your spirit, And let none deal treacherously with
> the wife of his youth. For the Lord God of Israel says that He
> hates divorce. . ." (Mal. 2:15-16a)

Let us not forget that the Great Commission requires the discipleship of the nations (Matt. 28:18-20). When most people think of the
word "nation," they take it to mean gigantic nation states, not small
tribes, cultural units, and families. When the first individuals and
households were baptized in the book of Acts, they were referred to
as disciples. These were people willing to be discipled on a regular
basis in the teachings of Jesus Christ. They were first baptized, and
then they were discipled. Similarly, our children are baptized and
then they are discipled in our homes with the expectation that the
Holy Spirit will work in their lives to regenerate and sanctify them
by the truth.

Purpose #3 - Dominion

The third purpose of the family is an economic component. I will
take this topic up in another chapter. However, carefully consider
the words of the following text:

> "And the Lord God said, "It is not good that man should be
> alone; I will make him a helper comparable to him." (Gen.
> 2:18)

Note that the word the Lord God chose to describe the woman's
role was not "companion" or "friend" or "sexual pleasure partner."
The primary purpose for the creation of Eve was to give Adam a helper for his accomplishment of the dominion task. He was given a job
to do, and she was there to help him with it. This is the beginning

of the family economy, an institution which has been largely lost in modern society. However, throughout this book, I hope to call Christians back to this fundamental building block of civilization and the kingdom of God. A better understanding of God's created purpose for man and woman would radically change the modern view of marriage and family.

Purpose #4 - Godly Fellowship and Christian Community

The fourth and final purpose for the Christian marriage and family is not mentioned very much in pre-marital counseling books and seminars on the family, but it is fundamental to life in Christ. Our relationships in the home are always assumed in Scripture to be taking place "in the Lord," as already mentioned (Col. 3:18, Eph. 6:1). Enmity and strife is the default position for the natural man who has not been reconciled to God through Jesus Christ (Isa. 48:22, 57:21, Jas. 4:4). It is only through Jesus Christ that we can be reconciled with God, and with each other, for Christ is our peace who has broken down all the middle walls of partition between us (Eph. 2:14). Christ is both the great Mediator between God and man, and the great Mediator between man and man. We are, therefore, the great community of the reconciled, the forgiven, and the forgiving. Christ stands between us holding both my hand and the hand of my Christian brother, and he places our hands together. Dietrich Bonhoeffer, in his classic work *Life Together*, writes,

> Without Christ we also would not know our brother, nor could we come to him. The way is blocked by our own ego. Christ opened up the way to God and to our brother. Now Christians can live with one another in peace; they can love and serve one another; they can become one.[16]

The Scriptures would have us to exhort each other daily, lest any be hardened with the deceitfulness of sin (Heb. 3:13). This daily theme will repeat itself throughout this book. Christians need each other on a regular basis. They need daily communion with each other, because we are the body of Christ. We receive Christ when we receive one another (Matt. 10:40, Rom. 15:7). This community is a God-sent gift every day and every time we interact with another Christian.

Even the sinning brother is seen as a forgiven brother. We are the fellowship of the forgiven. I have been forgiven by Christ and my brother has been forgiven by Christ, so of course I must forgive him too. Bonhoeffer again writes,

> Thus, the very hour of disillusionment with my brother becomes incomparably salutary, because it so thoroughly teaches me that neither of us can ever live by our own words and deeds, but only by that one Word and Deed which really binds us together—the forgiveness of sins in Jesus Christ.

These words are hugely encouraging and hopeful, given that we live in an impossibly sinful world, where sin is an ever-present reality and threat. The Christian marriage (and the Christian family), however becomes one of the greatest living realizations of the good news. The Lord Jesus Christ makes true spiritual life and relationship possible for the Christian. In the context of the Christian family that vitality comes to fuller bloom and produces an amazing testimony to the grace of God in the life of the soul.

So, what have we learned?

1. Why did Paul recommend singleness in 1 Corinthians 7?
2. What are the two important covenantal units to which a Christian single may belong?
3. What are the biblical and practical dangers of encouraging too much singleness?
4. What is the great mystery of marriage?
5. What is the difference between a head and a leader?

6. What are the specific duties emphasized for husbands and wives in Ephesians 5?
7. Why is the term "in the Lord" so important when it comes to these commands relating to marriage?
8. What is the connection between birth control, homosexuality, and pornography, according to Christian pastors in the 21st century?
9. What are the four purposes for which God designed the family?
10. How does Malachi 2:15 differ from the purpose for family outlined in the Noahic covenant and the creation mandate?

So, how are we doing?

1. On a scale of one to ten, how have we cultivated our marriage unity in the areas of:
   - Communication
   - Intimacy
   - Economics
   - Ministry
   - Bible Study
   - Worship
2. What are the misconceptions of family that we have had in the past, in comparison with the four biblical purposes for the family outlined in this chapter?
3. In what situations might it be appropriate to use birth control and to purposefully avoid having children?
4. How has your relationship with Christ affected your marriage? How does it affect your child raising?

5. In what situations are you as a husband seriously challenged when trying to love your wife as Christ loved the church? In what situations are you as a wife seriously challenged when trying to submit to your husband in the Lord?

6. How have you realized the four purposes for the family in your own home? Which was more of a surprise to you, as you read through this chapter?

2 FAMILY RELATIONSHIPS

*And you, fathers, do not provoke your children to wrath, but bring
them up in the training and admonition of the Lord.* (Eph. 6:4)

This chapter will focus upon the discipleship vision inculcated in
Ephesians 6:4. The time has never been better for the Christian
Church to realize this important principle!

As of 2014, only 27% of the Millennial Generation (18-38 years of
age) were attending church. That represents a decrease of 51% from
the church attendance rate of the Silent Generation.[18] Only 19% of
younger millennials call themselves evangelicals, down from 30%
for the Silent Generation.[19]

Church attendance is not the only indication of faithful adher-
ence to God's Word. Recent surveys have found that 44% of American evangelical millennials support homosexual marriage (what
the Apostle Paul describes as the radically "unnatural use" of sex-

uality).[20] This means that participation in conservative evangelicalism has declined to roughly 10% of the American population. Unless there is something of a revival in this country, Christianity is on the same trajectory as England, Scotland, Sweden, and Germany. The faith is slowly disappearing from these once-Christian nations. It is a generational leak that began with the Baby Boom generation and carried into the Gen-Xers and then to the Millennials.

Why the steady drift away from the faith, generation by generation? It is a question of discipleship. Ordinarily, I would argue that Christian families should expect to see continuity in the faith from generation to generation. This is the essential message of Malachi 4:6. Speaking of John the Baptist and the exciting introduction of the Messiah, Malachi says,

> "Behold, I will send you Elijah the prophet before the coming of the great and dreadful day of the Lord. And he will turn the hearts of the fathers to the children, and the hearts of the children to their fathers, lest I come and strike the earth with a curse." (Mal. 4:5-6)

Notice that the turning of the hearts to the faith of the fathers is the means by which the curse is averted. Malachi is speaking of the powerful work of the Holy Spirit of God in the New Testament era. The prophet Joel also speaks of the Holy Spirit poured out upon our "sons and daughters" (Joel 2:28). How then does this comport with the terrible lapse in faithfulness, generation by generation, seen over the last fifty years? While we do not want to ignore in any way God's sovereign hand over all things, there must be some modern phenomenon that contributes to this. What has changed in the discipleship of children over these last four to five generations?

Several things come to mind.

1. The state has aggressively promoted its secular education in Russia, China, and the Western countries. This statist, hu-

manist approach is relatively new in the history of the Western world, and it must be taken into account when considering the reasons for this generational apostasy. In many nations (like China, Russia, Sweden, Norway, and Germany), parents and churches would be breaking the law if they attempted to provide any religious instruction to children under 18 years of age.[21] This was the catalyst for much of the major Christian persecutions of the 20th and 21st centuries.

2. Powerful cultural influences arose during the 20th century that never existed previously in the history of the world. Almost every teenager in America who owns a smart phone with internet access is plugged into the Hollywood and Nashville worldviews. These powerful influences dictate ideologies, manners, cultures, and preferences in a very monolithic form. This mass media holds a thousand times more influence over the average teenaged child than it did in 1900.

3. Daily parental discipleship was marginalized in the homes of many Christians, due to the rise of a professional class of teachers in the church who were expected to provide the religious instruction. To the reasoning of some Christian parents, these traditions may very well have "made the commandment of God of no effect" (Matt. 15:6b).

It is the combination of the above factors that created the problem. When our young teens are immersed in thirty hours of a secular, godless education enforced by government fiat, mixed with thirty hours of contact with pop culture, along with a few hours of peer influence in a church youth group once a week, they will almost certainly align themselves with the ideals of pop culture and school. This is even more so the case if there is little or no contact with Christ in the home throughout the week.

Jesus said, "A disciple is not above his teacher, but everyone who is perfectly trained will be like his teacher" (Luke 6:40). Thus, Christ would pose this question to every parent as a follow-up: "Who have *you* assigned as the person(s) to disciple your children throughout the week?" No doubt, most parents haven't even considered this question, and herein lies the problem. By default, the system used to disciple most children (and their parents have hardly noticed) will be Lady Gaga, Charles Darwin, and Stephen Spielberg.

Responsibilities

Biblically speaking, the primary responsibility for the discipleship of children lies with the father, as indicated in Ephesians 6:4. Naturally, the father may delegate some of it to others. From passages like Proverbs 31, it is clear that mothers also play an important role in the discipleship of their sons (and daughters). The ultimate responsibility, however, still rests with the father. When the general manager of a company delegates a project to a middle manager, he will hold him responsible for the project. Should the man report back to him that the project is incomplete because of some lapse among his employees, the general manager is not going to take it up with the other employees. He will face the middle manager to whom he assigned the project with his failure, and discipline him accordingly. Plainly, God has assigned the child-raising department of the home to the father and He will hold the man responsible. If there is a problem, He will not call mother in to the "front office." Nor will He call up the Sunday School teacher. He will refer His concerns to the father.

We should not reject the contributions of the church or the preaching of the Word by the church, for all of that is important in the life of the child. And, it is the responsibility of the father to make sure his family is hearing the preaching of the Word. If discipleship is a matter of contact hours and daily interaction, then the primary disciplers will be those in contact with the disciple on a daily basis. Ordinarily, this discipleship would fall under fathers and mothers unless peers, pop culture, and public schools have somehow displaced parents in the equation.

When parents abdicate their Ephesians 6:4 responsibilities and turn them over to more powerful influences throughout the week, a thirty-minute Sunday School instruction cannot possibly compensate. Can we honestly call this Christian education or Christian discipleship of our children? Half-hearted efforts show a lack of commitment either in the parents or the church leadership, or both.

As I was raised on the mission field in Japan, "church" was an every-day event for us. For one thing, our tiny church met in our home on Sundays and it was an all-day affair. From morning until evening, we were in the Word, in fellowship, or in prayer, with services in Japanese and English. Throughout the week, my father would gather us together in the mornings to read the Bible, sing hymns and psalms, memorize verses and catechisms, and even listen to sermons on occasion. My mother would read to us from great Christian writers like John Bunyan and George Whitefield. This daily discipleship formed the six of us children more than the formal academic courses our parents assigned for us, which were also part of our education.

My father was doggedly consistent in this discipleship. I don't remember ever skipping daily time in the Word during these growing-up years. Even while on an overnight ferry trip to the northern Japanese island of Hokkaido, I can remember Dad officiating a time of family devotions. Dad wasn't always highly inspirational or emotionally connective in his discipleship. But he was self-controlled, disciplined, steady, and relentlessly consistent. After many years, I find my father to be the most frugal and generous men I've ever known. He loaded each of us with a library of the best Christian books money can buy before we left his home to start our own families. And, though I don't think his income ever topped the Federal Poverty Threshold, I'm sure he has given away more money than he ever spent. Today, Dad is in his 80s and he still heats his home with wood he cuts and splits himself.

Biblical Discipleship

Discipleship may conjure up a lot of different things in people's minds, but it is better to think of it in biblical terms.

1. Biblical discipleship takes place in a context or an atmosphere where the Word of Christ predominates. In our homes, we want to see our children swimming in God's forgiveness and God's goodness, where the teachings of Jesus Christ are presumed, mentioned, acted upon, and realized on a constant basis.

> "...Be filled with the Spirit, speaking to one another in psalms and hymns and spiritual songs, singing and making melody in your heart to the Lord, giving thanks always for all things to God the Father in the name of our Lord Jesus Christ." (Eph. 5:18b-20)

> "Let the word of Christ dwell in you richly in all wisdom, teaching and admonishing one another in psalms and hymns and spiritual songs, singing with grace in your hearts to the Lord. And whatever you do in word or deed, do all in the name of the Lord Jesus, giving thanks to God the Father through Him." (Col. 3:16-17)

The phenomenon described in Acts 2:41-47 must not be seen as exceptional, that is only belonging to the New Testament Church. It is normative to the Church of Jesus Christ from A.D. 33 to the present, wherever the bona fide Church has survived. The Christian family should be characterized by daily gladness, unity, praising of God, and "continuing steadfastly in the Apostle's doctrine and prayers."

Given that these people in Acts 2 were baptized, and given that our children are baptized and committed to discipleship, we should continue in the discipleship program Jesus instituted in the Great Commission.

This is the default position for Christian life and discipleship. Notice that corporate singing of psalms and hymns, and the teachings of Christ are preeminent. This is what will create the right atmosphere of discipleship in the home.

Biblical discipleship and Christian living will integrate God's Word into the fabric of life. This is the idea so beautifully conveyed through Deuteronomy 6:7-9. Again, the context is the home and the family.

> "You shall teach them diligently to your children, and shall talk of them when you sit in your house, when you walk by the way, when you lie down, and when you rise up. You shall bind them as a sign on your hand, and they shall be as frontlets between your eyes. You shall write them on the doorposts of your house and on your gates." (Deut. 6:7-9)

The key is integration. God's Word should be as a frontlet (or a constant inscribed reminder) that hangs between the eyes of the child. It is integrated into every bodily position the child finds himself in—sitting, walking, lying down, and rising up. Every way the child turns, he is confronted with the true and living God, His Christ, and His Word. This discipleship involves intentional times of teaching (where God's Word are written on the doorposts and the walls), and extemporaneous opportunities (where we speak of these things as we "walk by the way").

God's Word must run in the bloodstream of the home, always and ever. We pray without ceasing (1 Thess. 5:16). It should go without saying that we would not want to place our children anywhere that extemporaneous prayer is illegal, unless of course we were in a prison camp where we had no control over our children's raising. There is hardly any more obvious application to the mandate: "We ought to obey God rather than men."

A young Christian lady was babysitting a four-year-old child from another Christian home. When something delightful occurred, the young lady suggested they thank the Lord for it. The little child replied, "We only do that on Sundays." This is only one small anecdote that illustrates a powerfully-ingrained mindset. Many professing Christians today share this view of faith in that their faith is not integrated into life. It is a highly compartmentalized faith, largely irrelevant to life, and to that extent, non-existent. This is the major cause for the dying of the faith in the West. Each successive generation eventually gets the message. The faith is unimportant, irrelevant, and lifeless.

There are many different ways to integrate God's Word into the day; our family utilizes these practical examples, and more:

- I sit down at the piano spontaneously throughout the day and play well known hymns, singing and making melody to the Lord. Several of my children usually end up joining me.
- We sing together before almost every meal, usually one of five different songs that make up our "family liturgy." Typically, we revert to Psalm 89, Psalm 23, "This is the Day the Lord Has Made," Ephesians 4:32, "To God Be the Glory," and "It Is Well With My Soul."
- Every conflict is an opportunity for humility, confession, forgiveness, and prayer. I try to seize these opportunities as often as they arise. Without exception, we find spiritual growth and great peace come out of it.
- While helping my daughter with her physics lessons I burst out into prayer on occasion, praising God for His amazing creation. References to God, and prayers giving glory to God,

are few and far between in most science textbooks written for Christian home schools. Christian parents must improvise as they teach these subjects.

- When we watch a video together, our family will always insert commentary, biblical truths, and reproof for any unfruitful works of darkness. One of the reasons why I developed "The World View in Five Minutes"[22] and trained my daughters to write and edit these segments for the radio broadcast was so that I could teach them to interpret news and world events by a biblical worldview. I wanted them to see all of life through the interpretive lens of Scripture, which defines reality by the sovereignty of God and by the revealed laws of God that determine our ethics. They need to see that these world events are not primarily effects of random causes in a materialist universe, or even man-caused forces. They are the very acts of God.

2. In any form of discipleship, more is caught than taught. Back in 2015, the Generations ministry released a study on the present apostasy of an entire generation, an apostasy unprecedented in the history of this nation (this study is reviewed in the appendix of this book). Our team studied the phenomenon through an extensive survey of four influences in a young person's life: parental relationships, education methodology, church, and popular culture. Of the hundreds of metrics our data analysts looked at, the most dramatic correlation was seen between the apostasy of the child and the hypocrisy of the parents. We were asking young people the question, "Do your parents' lives and actions make you more likely to adopt their religious standard and specific beliefs?" When parents say one thing and do another, their children will most often take note of it and reject the things they say (especially if it bears anything of a Christian character). In effect, their children are only living out a more consistent life

of apostasy than that which their parents held to. As each successive generation of faith since 1930 has grown weaker in this country, church-going parents often initiate the apostasy while their children complete it.

Parents, therefore, would do well to make their calling and election sure (2 Pet. 1:10), and make sure that their love is without hypocrisy (Rom. 12:9). Honestly consider areas of inconsistency, and assess your true priorities by the actual use of your time and resources. Have you cultivated an external religion, having a form but denying the power thereof? When you see sinful tendencies arise in your children's lives, you should double check to see if the seed of that sin was first rooted in your life. When a father is given to pornography and self-gratification, he should not be surprised to see homosexuality in the life of his son or daughter. The father that cannot submit to church leadership (as evidenced by church-hopping and general rebellion) will most likely see rebellion surface in his own children. Parents who speak dishonorably of their own parents will more than likely find their children treating them the same way. Bursts of anger, simmering bitterness, and wrathful, controlling fathers and mothers may even see see their own children committing murder. Parents who are given to the idolatrous use of food, entertainment, and sensuality should not be surprised when they discover their children are addicted to drugs and alcohol. Faithless talk, constant anxiety, and prayerlessness among parents would naturally lead to doubt and all-out skepticism in their children.

Oftentimes, our children's sin appears more pronounced and this can serve well as a magnifying glass to reveal the real issues that lie under the surface in our own lives. Thankfully, this is never the end of the story. God brings these crises into our lives to wake us up to our further need for Christ.

We will never pass on a generational heritage of sinless perfection to our children. There is no better generational vision than that of a father and mother who fears God and passes on a heritage of humble repentance to their children. Our children need to see a brokenness in us. They need to hear us confessing our sin before God and others around us. As the Word of God impacts us, we undergo a radical change of perspective towards ourselves, towards sin, righteousness, God, and Christ's tremendous work. If they see greater transparency in us, and a greater openness to exhortation from others in the church body, they are likely to follow our example.

There have been periods of hardness of heart in my home, but I thank God there are also times of refreshing. Hearts break and tears pour out, as heartfelt confessions come from Dad, Mom, and the children. This is the only hope for a sinful home.

Relationship vs. Love

"Relationship" is a new buzzword that shows up everywhere in Christian as well as non-Christian contexts. Christian churches say they want to be "all about relationship." Family ministries abound in this country organized for the stated purpose of "strengthening relationships." As used by many modern systems of education and scientific fields, words become slippery things and they can obscure the truth rather than reveal it. Varying connotations come attached to the word "relationship," and it takes on a sentimental value that helps when marketing a ministry.

Actually, the word "relationship" doesn't really mean much. If we're talking human sociology, relationship is only a context in which human beings come into contact with each other. It bears no real ethical value, because two humans may be in a good relationship or a bad relationship. But then, one is still left with distinguishing good and bad! It is much better to use biblical terms that are given biblical definition, revealed by God to us (so we don't get lost in our human-derived "psycho-babble.")

Of course, the Bible encourages us to love, and then God provides in clear terms what that love will look like. Homosexuals say they have great relationships and they speak of love. Increasingly, families who claim good relationships fall into incest. Rudyard Kipling spoke of the one "who started by loving his neighbor, and ended by loving his wife." It seems that we do need biblical definitions to help us here. God's commandments show us what loving our neighbor looks like.

> Owe no one anything except to love one another, for he who loves another has fulfilled the law. For the commandments, "You shall not commit adultery," "You shall not murder," "You shall not steal," "You shall not bear false witness," "You shall not covet," and if there is any other commandment, are all summed up in this saying, namely, "You shall love your neighbor as yourself." Love does no harm to a neighbor; therefore love is the fulfillment of the law. (Rom. 13:8-10)

People like to speak of love and relationships in nebulous terms, but they usually wind up destroying their relationships when they do so. An over-focus on the relational context is usually self-oriented. We're thinking about ourselves when we are gauging how close we are to this person or that person. If we status the relationship by how well we know each other, this gives us very little data as to the true state of that relationship. Mere intention to build relationship and community sets us up for disappointment and defrauding. We set up expectations and then crush them.

1 Corinthians 13 also provides a clear definition of *agape* love. While we may insist that we love in some superficial sense, God's Word gives us a metric by which to measure the genuineness of that love. Did we love to the point of sacrifice? Did love seek its own at

all yesterday? Did love suffer long? Was our love rude and insensitive even a little? Did love bear all things, believe all things, hope all things, and endure all things? An honest assessment of our love by the 1 Corinthians 13 standard on a regular basis is the best gauge of the state of our family relationships.

This love cannot be truly lived out by anybody short of them receiving the love of God. When I meet children that exhibit extraordinary love towards their friends at church or school, I think to myself: "I would sure like to meet their parents. What sort of loving parents would have taught a child like this to love?" Only those who have received the profoundest love can share that love with anybody else. Merely witnessing that love at a distance is not enough. You have to be a recipient of that love in the family of God to exhibit the supernatural love of God. This is what John tells us in his first epistle:

> "In this is love, not that we loved God, but that He loved us and sent His Son to be the propitiation for our sins. Beloved, if God so loved us, we also ought to love one another. No one has seen God at any time. If we love one another, God abides in us, and His love has been perfected in us." (1 John 4:10-12)

Families and church communities that desire closeness will often construct "community" and "relationship" before they have learned to love. They expect that love will fill that capacity for relationship. They may assume they are the greatest of lovers, but they fail to define love biblically.

There are three elements that test our love: proximity of other people, time, and conflict (or suffering). Isolation from other people truly does exempt us from the call for love, and this is the problem of modern man. He holes himself away in a hermetically-sealed container so there is little contact with "other people." In the words of the great existentialist, Jean-Paul Sartre, "Hell is other people." Thus, every individual in the home plugs himself into his own iPod, iPhone, and iLife. The children are shuffled into daycare, preschool, and other anonymous forms of life-sans-relationship. And everybody gets along reasonably well as long as they don't run into each other in the hallway. Given the context of relationship, sufficient time, and opportunity for conflicts (or suffering), love will either express itself or it will not. If love does not show up on the scene, then estrangement, divorce, disownment, and emancipation will be the inevitable result. The world does its level best to avoid true relationships through transience or constant relocation, through isolation, and through recurrent breaking of relationship. Conflict in the home and the church is the best test of true Christian love and true Christian forgiveness. While biblical conflict resolution, peacemaking, and forgiveness is fairly foreign to post-modern life, these things will occasionally be found in a Christian home or a Christian church.

We must be careful not to manufacture a relational context merely for the sake of the context, without the love to reside there. Some parents not given to self-sacrificial love, humility, and forgiveness believe they have close relationships with their children. They attempt to micro-manage the lives of their teens, or maintain tight control of their children's dating and courtship. The results are almost inevitably catastrophic. They misinterpret their "close relationships" to be filled with love. In point of fact, they have constructed a context for love, but love never really showed up! At the end of the day, they ruined more relationships by attempting closeness, accountability, and community without love. It might have been better if they had let their kids date and remained relatively uninvolved in their children's relationships, given the lack of love within their family.

We must be brutally honest in our assessment of our own love. Yes, we want sufficient love to fill the relationship context of our home and our covenant family. These are redemptive contexts for love, contexts for kingdom work, and contexts for discipleship. We want Christ to completely fill our relationships. Therefore, honesty and humility are most essential in our relationships. Let's admit it. We are not the greatest lovers in the world. When we come into contact with each other, we soon discover our true condition by nature, and it is not a pretty picture. That is where we see our need for Christ.

Humans are very good at creating wonderful facades and what appear on the outside to be well-ordered families that love each other. However, the most "mature" Christian families can turn out to be the most judgmental (violating Matthew 7:1-5), the most divisive, and the least loving at the end of the day. They may have created their relational contexts, attended seminars on courtship, led marriage workshops, and joined a family-integrated church that was "all about" family discipleship and family worship. But these turn out to be nothing but empty shells and facades where there is no love. Here's what the Apostle Paul would tell them:

> "Though I speak with the tongues of men and of angels, but have not love, I have become sounding brass or a clanging cymbal. And though I have the gift of prophecy, and understand all mysteries and all knowledge, and though I have all faith, so that I could remove mountains, but have not love, I am nothing. And though I bestow all my goods to feed the poor, and though I give my body to be burned, but have not love, it profits me nothing." (1 Cor. 13:1-4)

Here are some practical steps towards creating a sincere love without hypocrisy (Rom. 12:9) in the home:

1) Test your own selflessness in the relationship. Have you pressed for closeness in the relationship, but failed to love selflessly all along (according to the 1 Corinthians 13 model)? Closeness in relationship should naturally follow the presence of love. Also, 1 Corinthians 13 teaches us that, "Love is not rude." Biblical love does not create expectations it cannot fulfill.

Some homeschooling families, for example, discover that the mother-son dynamic can be counterproductive to healthy relationships, especially through the teen years. Fathers and husbands should be sensitive to this. It can be an unloving thing to force a mother and son together for seven-24 hour days for 18 years straight.

2) Keeping God's commandments is more important than form and context. The Bible does not command a certain regimen for the introduction of young people into marriage. Numbers 30 allows a father vow-veto power, but the text does not require some particular minimum level of involvement for a father in the courtship of his daughter. In some cases, the father chooses not to get involved, and his daughter doesn't really want his involvement. These are not essential matters. What really matters is this: Are we keeping the commandments of God? Here are several commands that tie into this preparation and introduction into marriage.

- Flee fornication.
- Love your neighbor (your daughter) as yourself.
- Honor your father and mother.
- Provoke not your daughter to wrath.
- Walk in the light.
- Judge not that ye be not judged.

Too seldom are the commandments of God reviewed when Christian families think about marriage. They are so busy working out their fences, their chaperones, and their own rules; or they just ignore every rule altogether and default to the decayed morals of the day.

Different families and cultures maintain different traditions, and we should allow liberty for various approaches to courtship, dating, etc. However, when it comes to extra-biblical systems and human traditions, Paul reminds us to keep the commandments of God before our eyes first and foremost:

> "Was anyone called while circumcised? Let him not become uncircumcised. Was anyone called while uncircumcised? Let him not be circumcised. Circumcision is nothing and uncircumcision is nothing, but keeping the commandments of God is what matters." (1 Cor. 7:18-19)

Christian families will apply God's principles in a myriad of ways, and we should allow for these differences in the way we think about each other. The same thing applies to education, family culture, etc. What matters most of all is that we are loving God, loving our neighbor as ourselves, and obeying the commandments of God.

3) Most importantly, a sincere love for one another begins with a true love for God. Where there is no love for God, there cannot be true love for the others in the home. Why do "Christian" parents fail to teach their children God's Word (in accordance with Deuteronomy 6:7) on a daily basis? Taking in the context for this passage, we read:

> "Hear, O Israel: The Lord our God, the Lord is one! You shall love the Lord your God with all your heart, with all your soul, and with all your strength. And these words which I command you today shall be in your heart. You shall teach them diligently to your children. . ."

The quintessential demonstration of our love for God, according to this passage, is the communication of it from the heart of the parent to the children. First, however, a father must know the love that God has shown him in the Lord Jesus Christ. If he has received that love, then of course he will love God and share the One that he loves above everything else to the children he loves. This is the basis for love and discipleship in the home.

How We Want to Characterize Our Family Relationships

"Now the works of the flesh are evident, which are: adultery, fornication, uncleanness, lewdness, idolatry, sorcery, hatred, contentions, jealousies, outbursts of wrath, selfish ambitions, dissensions, heresies, envy, murders, drunkenness, revelries, and the like; of which I tell you beforehand, just as I also told you in time past, that those who practice such things will not inherit the kingdom of God. But the fruit of the Spirit is love, joy, peace, longsuffering, kindness, goodness, faithfulness, gentleness, self-control. Against such there is no law." (Gal. 5:19-23)

The difference between a Christian family and a non-Christian family should be obvious, or easily evident, as the above text says. What is it that characterizes our homes? If we are Christians, all of us have the Spirit of God. "Now if anyone does not have the Spirit of Christ, he is not His" (Rom. 8:9). Should a non-Christian be reading this and find that verses 19-21 characterize his life more than verses 22 and 23, I encourage him or her to be honest about the absence of grace. Be honest about the sin that dominates your life, and sincerely cry out to God for mercy. Believe in the Lord Jesus Christ who saves you from the wretched condition of sin and you will be saved, and your household (Acts 16:31).

A mother that loves her children will want to lead them to Jesus, especially when she sees behavioral issues arise in them. She treats her children with kindness and gentleness, and she does not give way to sinful anger. A father that loves his sons and daughters will get into the habit of sacrificing time and energy for them. He will find ways to show affection and affirmation to his teen daughters, even when they are pushing him away. He will write letters to them. He will quietly and thoughtfully counsel them through their emotional struggles. He will affirm them with affectionate words, and show them appropriate affection. He will pray for his children, sometimes for hours at a time. He refuses to respond in kind to hurtful words that come from his own wife or one of his children. These are examples of how the fruit of love reveals itself in the home.

Loving a two-year-old will be very different from loving a sixteen-year old. Thus, I find that I must relearn "love" every ten years or so. In God's incomprehensible yet beautiful purposes, He rewrites the lessons so as to better teach us to love one another. He breaks us out of our comfort zone, which is typically a self-oriented frame of thinking.

We must learn new ways to communicate, and to communicate love. When I was having a hard time communicating with one of my daughters, I took up playing tennis with her. By praising her serves and her returns, and talking through the entire practice session I found that I could speak my heart and she would listen to me. Every father must learn how to cross the communication barriers, and speak love to his sons and daughters.

Our relationships are characterized by joy, because we see our children walking in the truth (3 John 4). Every indication of the Spirit's work is cause for celebration. Unless our "grace antennas" are well calibrated to sense any work of grace, our homes will not be characterized by gratefulness and joy. If all we see is the devil's work, sinful behavior, and a failure to meet our own expectations, we will not sense the grace of God when He is working in our children's lives.

The Christian home is a peaceful home, where there is more peacemaking than peace-breaking. Conflict is inevitable, at some level. However, the overriding atmosphere of the home is peaceful. Peacemakers (Jesus followers) desire peace and seek peace. We do not let the sun go down upon our wrath (Eph. 4:26). Where fathers and husbands, and mothers and wives confess sin to the family and to God in prayer, there will be an atmosphere of peace. Families that interact with other families within the church fellowship will particularly find more opportunities to forgive others, and to demonstrate the peaceable fruit of righteousness. As Christians, we are almost always treated badly by the world, and by professing Christians too. When we respond graciously, without bitterness or gossip, Jesus Christ shines through us, and our families become even more peaceful and gracious.

Thus, the Christian home must be a humble home. The defensiveness, self-justifications, emotional manipulation, blame-shifting, rivalries, and judgmentalism that make so many families contentious today all come from pride. Pride is an inaccurate perspective of oneself in reference to God (1 Pet. 5:5-6). The problem with modern man is not lack of self-esteem—it is a lack of God esteem. Once we have secured a more accurate esteem for God, then we will retain a more appropriate esteem for ourselves and others. When we see God's standard of holiness and see our low and pitiful condition in reference to God, we can hardly compare ourselves to each other anymore.

If there is a single gift from God that is always the foundation of a happy home, I think it is humility. One popular music artist from the 1960s wrote a song that identified the problem with many a marriage in the present day. "It's my belief pride is the chief cause in the decline in the number of husbands and wives."

A humble father will be careful not to hold his son or daughter to a standard he would never have held to himself at the same age or under similar circumstances. He becomes a good listener, slow to speak, quick to hear, and slow to anger. He is correctable himself, especially when the elders of the church come for a home visit. Mothers set a beautiful example of meekness when they submit themselves to their husbands with cheerfulness instead of grumbling, arguing, nit-picking, and sniping. These are true fruits of the Spirit of God in the life of the Christian family.

To be long-suffering is to maintain a good attitude while suffering for a very long time. It's really that simple, but it's not easy. When we suffer whether it be from disease or persecution from family members or friends, we learn to respond as Jesus responded to His sufferings. The life of Christ shines through us and our children see it. They hear us repeating the words of Jesus, "Oh Father, not my will, but Thine be done!" They hear us crying out, "Father, forgive them for they know not what they do!" Of all the lessons we teach our children, I think this is the most powerful. The way my father reacted to suffering, especially when he lost almost half of his missionary support in the mid-1970s, impacted his children for a lifetime. My mother would always commend my father's steadfast, grateful, uncomplaining attitude during those years. He found a way to purchase bread crusts from bakeries in Japan for cents on the dollar during those tight years. (Typically, the Japanese would not eat the bread crusts—what they called the "ears" of the loaves.) So we had plenty to eat, as long as we were willing to thank the Lord for the provision of bread crusts! It is a father's attitude when he faces a job loss or other difficult trial that speaks the loudest to his children.

Our homes should be characterized by kindness. Our family's favorite song is taken word for word from Ephesians 4:32:

> "Be ye kind one to another, tender hearted, forgiving one another even as God for Christ's sake has forgiven you."

We have sung this chorus in our home almost every day for 25 years. If you would like the tune for it, just call our home and one of the children will sing it for you. Singing a song 10,000 times will not necessarily produce kindness, but it does remind us of the kindness and forgiveness of Jesus. It sets a tone for our home. It brings us back to what our home is all about; the kindness of Jesus Christ. Love is not rude, and it should be sensitive to that which might offend our brothers and sisters in the home and the church. Even so, we cannot say, "I didn't mean to offend your sensitivities." We have an obliga-tion to know the things that may or may not offend others around us, but this doesn't preclude loving admonitions and rebukes if some-body is habitually falling into sin. However, our day-to-day inter-actions with each other should not be characterized by harshness, sarcasm, teasing, or demeaning jokes. Relationships obligate us to know something of each other before we speak in certain ways. What some might take as kindness and consideration, others might receive as an insult.

All of these fruits serve as real tests of the quality of a Spirit-filled life in the home. It turns out that the family is the best test of that Spirit life. It forces us to be honest with ourselves. Is there a work of grace in our lives or not? We live in a day where false fronts and false professions are so common, that we are pressed to seek an honest answer to this question.

So... what have we learned?

1. How is the curse reverted, according to Malachi 4:6? Who are the "fathers" mentioned here?
2. What modern phenomenon has contributed to the serious generational downgrade in the faith?
3. To whom, specifically, does the Bible delegate the discipleship of children? Reference the key passages.
4. What is the Acts 2 vision for the Christian community/fellow-ship? How were the early Christians spending their days?
5. How does Deuteronomy 6:7-9 describe the integration of God's Word into life?
6. What is the difference between relationship and love?
7. What are the key passages in Scripture that describe love in clear terms?

8. What are the specific commandments of God that are relevant to courtship and dating?
9. What is the true motive for Deuteronomy 6:7 discipleship, as laid out in Deuteronomy 6:4?
10. Which of the fruits of the Spirit are best seen as they operate within the context of relationships, especially family relationships?
11. Which of the fruits of the Spirit are best manifested during times of trial and affliction?

So... how are we doing?

1. How are the fruits of the Spirit manifesting themselves in your home (or your living situation)? At the very least, try to address love, joy, peace, longsuffering, kindness, and humility.
2. What is the difference between loving a two-year-old child versus loving an eighteen-year-old young man or young woman, or an 85-year-old grandmother?

3 FAMILY DEVOTION

Let not thine heart envy sinners: but be thou in the fear of the LORD all the day long. (Prov. 23:17, KJV)

Every household in every culture around the world lives with a certain orientation that governs the general attitude, goals, priorities, and life of that household. This orientation is foundational to everything else. *It is a fear, a reverence, and a worship for something or somebody.* Most unbelieving households in our culture live in the fear, the reverence, and the worship of money and materials, of power and popular opinion. Pagan households in times past lived in the fear of the spirits or the gods. It should not be difficult to trace the entire attitude of the home, along with its goals, priorities, and activities back to this one question: Whom or what do you fear? Who or what has got you in its grip?

For the Christian, the fear of God is the beginning of wisdom and knowledge of everything. This includes knowledge concerning sin, salvation, and the death and resurrection of Christ. Without the fear of God, these things mean nothing to the mind of the natural man.

We could not possibly develop a biblical perspective of the family without this foundational consideration. When the psalms set out to describe the godly vision for family, this characteristic is mentioned first:

> "Praise the Lord! Blessed is the man who fears the Lord, who delights greatly in His commandments. His descendants will be mighty on earth; the generation of the upright will be blessed." (Psalm 112:1-2)

> "Blessed is every one who fears the Lord, who walks in His ways. When you eat the labor of your hands, you shall be happy, and it shall be well with you. Your wife shall be like a fruitful vine in the very heart of your house, your children like olive plants all around your table. Behold, thus shall the man be blessed who fears the Lord." (Psalm 128:1-4)

The God-fearing household is the God-blessed household. This is where all the blessings begin. Naturally, this calls for belief that God really is "a rewarder of those that diligently seek Him" (Heb. 11:6). When my children reflect on their father, I want them to see a man who was always willing to put his entire fortune, his entire reputation, his ministries, and his position on the line for one politically-incorrect message—one unpopular stance that still accords with God's standard of righteousness. My father lost half of his support on the mission field when he suggested to his support base in the States that God was sovereign over every aspect of reality and truth. He wrote books on the sovereignty of God and six-day Creation—not exactly the most popular topics among Christian churches in the

1970s. He sincerely believed that this was God's truth, and for Dad, the fear of God trumped everything. I believe this was the most defining moment in the life of my father's ministry (especially for his family). All six children have steadfastly maintained a strong allegiance to these doctrines, and continue to serve the Lord in various Christian churches around the world to this day.

Popular opinion swings wildly from one extreme to another. Materials come and go. Churches are here today and gone tomorrow. Success is a slippery thing in this world. There is no more potent, more stabilizing, more defining, or more blessed contribution we can make to our children's lives, than to live before them in the fear of God all the day long, for thirty, forty, or fifty years.

The fear of the true and living God is the best fear of them all. It dispels all fear of circumstances, mitigating anxieties. It displaces any fear of relationships and codependency. We should be more afraid of offending God than we are of offending our children in the case that they need correction or restraint. This was where Eli went wrong with his sons, and consequently his family was subjected to the imprecation of God (1 Sam. 2:29, 3:13). There is no downside to the fear of God in our homes. In fact, we are promised that this fear of God offers the best possible security for our children. The most stable households are the ones that fear God.

"In the fear of the Lord there is strong confidence, and His children will have a place of refuge." (Prov. 14:26)

Let us also remember that this fear of God is the fear, love, honor, and reverence due a Father. We fear the "God and Father of our Lord Jesus Christ" (Eph. 1:3). It is no craven fear, for we know the Father if we have come to know the Son through the Gospel (John 14:7-9).

What This Fear Looks Like

One of the ways that we live out this fear before our children is by defending the Father's Name. We react strongly against any irreverence towards the Name of God (Ex. 20:7). In my youth, I remember that my father would carefully mark out minced oaths in some of our children's books. Whenever authors would use the word "gosh" for "God," or "darn" for "damn," or "heck" for "hell," my father recognized these words as God's sacred name and works. It is God's prerogative to damn things to hell, and the judgment of God ought never to be treated lightly. These are the little things that children never forget. When our Lord referred to the Father, He prayed to his "Holy Father" (John 17). In His instruction on praying, He has instructed us to "hallow" the name of our Father. Rushing through the name of God in our prayers, using the name in a thoughtless, repetitive, and reckless manner, ought to be avoided. Our children will mainly hear of the fear of God as it is patterned by their father or mother in prayer. Actually, over the years you will find that your children will generally pray as you have prayed, using the same words and inflections that they have heard you use. Will they learn to fear God in your household?

> "Come, you children, listen to me; I will teach you the fear of the Lord." (Ps. 34:11)

Thanksgiving

Before Paul launches into his admonitions concerning the family in Colossians 3, he carries out a line of thinking that is instructive for us to follow. He is speaking to Christians here, those who have been baptized into Christ. He says, "We have been raised with Christ, and we have died with Him, and our life is now hidden with Christ in God" (vv. 1-4). That is our new position. Henceforth, we are all empowered to put on tender mercies, kindness, humility, meekness, and longsuffering, providing forgiveness for each other all the day long (v. 12). That is our new life in Christ. The words that summarize this new life from day to day are found in verses 16 and 17:

> "Let the word of Christ dwell in you richly in all wisdom, teaching and admonishing one another in psalms and hymns and spiritual songs, singing with grace in your hearts to the Lord. And whatever you do in word or deed, do all in the name of the Lord Jesus, giving thanks to God the Father through Him."

From here on out, it is a life of singing and gratitude! If the fear of God is the concrete in the foundation of the home, thanksgiving is the drywall, the furnishings, and the window coverings of the home. We thank the Lord for one another, precious souls loved by Christ and saved by His blood. We experience a perpetual relief from sins forgiven, joy of divine reconciliation, and an acceptance into the family of God. We are thankful for each blessing, each relationship, all evidences of life (spiritual and physical), our eternal inheritance, God's majestic creation, the water, the sun, the air we breathe, physical protection, and every sign of His kingdom. In the darkest days, we thank the Lord for every glimmer of light and every evidence of His goodness.

Years ago, I was on a ministry trip with one of my daughters, and it happened that I was particularly concerned for her spiritual life at that time. Waking up at 3:00 in the morning, I lay in bed in anguish of spirit and poured out my petitions to God for her. It was at that moment that she murmured the name of Jesus in her sleep, and I was instantly comforted. That was all I needed for encouragement at that moment, and I thanked the Lord for it: a glimmer of light, a cloud the size of man's hand. We thank God for the smallest blessings at every opportunity.

Sharing the Word

Christians cannot live without the Word, and we will not thrive without the mutual sharing and exhortation from the Word on a daily basis. This is essential for any Christian community anywhere in the world. Generally, the family is the best manifestation of this reality. Dietrich Bonhoeffer describes Christian community in these terms: "The Christian needs another Christian who speaks God's Word to him. He needs him again and again when he becomes uncertain and discouraged, for by himself he cannot help himself without belying the truth."[23] Bonhoeffer offers this distilled definition of Christian community, as does the writer to the Hebrews. It must be a daily community. "But exhort one another daily, while it is called 'Today,' lest any of you be hardened through the deceitfulness of sin." (Heb. 3:13)

This serious divine mandate should structure the Christian experience. It applies as much to the single Christian living alone as it does to the family. There isn't any "wiggle room" with this injunction and warning, and this is why Christians should live in proximity to other Christians.

My father took this biblical principle seriously, and our family enjoyed a time of worship every morning from 7:20 a.m. to 8:00 a.m. If there was a single human factor I could point to that yielded good fruit among all six children in our home, it was the consistent application of this principle. Based on my experience as an elder and pastor over twenty years, where there are systemic problems within Christian families, there will be a lack of daily discipleship in the Word. In the present milieu of Christian superficiality, it is extremely rare to find families that actually get into the Word of God on a daily basis with an earnest desire for it. There are usually other priorities that squeeze it out. When asked how many born-again parents actually do family worship, the Christian pollster George Barna reported that only one in twenty have even tried it.[24]

About three years ago, I found my family drying out spiritually; relationships were a little stiff, there was little joy in our home, and sin seemed to be getting the upper hand. Although we had seldom missed time in the Word as a family each day, it had turned into a rote exercise—cursory and brief. This sense of spiritual barrenness is devastating and a critical problem, because it is a threat to our most vital relationship. That life-giving sustenance of the vine was sparse and tenuous. We knew that we had to do something drastic, and so I called for a three-month sabbatical. All of life's other priorities had to be set aside. We left our home, and spent time in rented condos and cabins off the grid. We extended our family devotion time to at least an hour a day. The important thing was to allow plenty of time for the Spirit to work in each of us, plenty of time for discussion, for confession, and prayer. Looking back, I think this was the most important practical element in our change of life priorities. God worked powerfully in our family during the following year. Change did not happen immediately, but gradually we could see the whole tenor of the family change from isolation to community, from heaviness to joy, and from a fixation on entertainment to an appreciation for the Word and worship. I called it "going to church" every day. For the first time in our family's experience, every day was like Sunday. We spent concerted time sitting at the feet of Christ each day, such that the daily work agenda did not dominate anymore. Martha did not interrupt Mary as she used to do. What a great change this brought about in our home! My wife and I more easily pray together throughout the day, and there is less distance between "the sacred" and "the secular."

The Basic Stuff

> "It is the Spirit who gives life; the flesh profits nothing. The words that I speak to you are spirit, and they are life. . . From that time many of His disciples went back and walked with Him no more. Then Jesus said to the twelve, "Do you also want to go away?" But Simon Peter answered Him, "Lord, to whom shall we go? You have the words of eternal life." (John 6:63, 66-68)

The Word of God is the very lifeblood of the family. It is our food and drink, and we cannot survive without it. Until the family (especially the husband and wife) sees the vital necessity of the ministry of the Word, there will be spiritually emaciated and hardened souls sitting around the living room. I would not want to impose any minimum time requirement, but I would recommend a consistent, daily regimen. This is the thrust of Hebrews 3:13. Fifteen minutes of daily time in the Word is better than an inconsistent hour-long convocation once or twice a week.

Several years ago, I asked my father if he had been discipled by his father. His response surprised me. He told me that his father had read the Bible faithfully to his family, but he didn't have a relationship with his father. Although traditional Christianity in the 1940s and 1950s typically maintained respect for the Scriptures, there was something stilted about the communication of God's Word in homes at that time. In some homes, the family Bible appeared prominently on the coffee table in the living room but it was never opened. Thankfully, there was still something of a viable heritage of faith in my family background.

However, the Word is meant to come alive. It is meant to be relevant to every situation. It is interesting that Ephesians 6:4 and Hebrews 13:3 do not simply instruct us to "read the Word." We are called to come along side and encourage each other through exhortations.

We are to apply the Word to the relevant needs of the present situation. Given that we have been in relationship and in communication with one another in the home, we should be able to make relevant applications.

Let's make this as simple as possible. We take up the Word and find an admonition in the Proverbs such as, "Go to the ant, you sluggard. Consider her ways and be wise." And so, we speak of the problem of slothfulness and how it affects our physical and spiritual life. We point out the work of Christ, who gave Himself for us in order that we might not henceforth live for ourselves but live for Him (2 Cor. 5:14). Then, we use the example of the diligent little ants. We note that these little creatures do not need a supervisor micro-managing their every activity. Nobody is telling the little ant to make his bed or do his school work. The ants appear to be self-motivated. Then, we think about ourselves. "Yesterday," you might say, "I noticed the kitchen waste basket was filled clear to the brim, and banana peels were falling on to the floor... and nobody took the initiative to empty it. I think we may have a problem with laziness in our family. This may be a problem with all of us, myself included." Then, you take a moment to confess this sin and ask for God's forgiveness in and through Jesus Christ. That is how to take relevant Scripture and apply it to your particular family's situation. This cannot be done by a Sunday School teacher or a pastor who sees the child for only thirty minutes each week. It is the parent who lives with the child who is best fitted to provide that personal discipleship.

Briefly, here is a summary of the most important elements of family discipleship.

1. Read the Bible, and draw out an exhortation. There are two words used in the New Testament that are translated "exhortation." The first word, *parakaleo* is used in Heb. 3:13 and Heb. 10:25, and it is to use the Word of God to come alongside somebody else so as to en-

courage them in their Christian walk. It can involve a call to repentance, or a call to duty (Acts 2:40). The second word is *noutheteo*; this word is more direct and is sometimes translated "admonishment." This is the word used for exhorting children in Eph. 6:4. (The word is also used for correcting the slothful in 1 Thess. 5:14 and 2 Thess. 3:14).

2. Integrate Bible teaching into your daily routines as you sit in the house, as you walk by the way, as you rise up, and as you lie down. Your teaching is extemporaneous at many points only because the situation throughout the day changes so rapidly. Should you notice a billboard on the highway sporting the Proverbs 7 woman (immodest and sensuously presented), why not turn that into a teaching opportunity using the Word? "Son, there's the Proverbs 7 woman. We don't want to have fellowship with the unfruitful works of darkness, but we should rather reprove them." This integration of biblical truth into life should come naturally, regularly, and relevantly to the situation that confronts us.

3. Encourage discussion and questions. Biblical discipleship is usually described in terms of these back-and-forth interactions (Ex. 12:26-27; 13:14; Deut. 6:20-25), something that my father found missing in his relationship with his father, though he was raised in a Christian home. If this is missing in a discipleship experience, it is time to reexamine the quality of the relationships.

4. Catechisms can also be a good way to teach biblical truths. This is less extemporaneous and more formal. It should not displace the informal, nor should it turn the discipleship into something stilted and irrelevant to life. Deuteronomy 6:7-9 commends both this formal teaching (where the Word is written on the posts and gates), and the informal, extemporaneous teaching as we "walk by the way." The benefit of catechisms such as the Westminster Shorter Catechism is that they provide a comprehensive summary of the

teachings of God's Word. We do not want our children leaving the home with giant gaps in their understanding of biblical truth, where they are subject to "every wind of doctrine and the cunning craftiness whereby men lay in wait to deceive" (Eph. 4:14). Most cults today grow by "evangelizing" children who were raised in Christian homes but were not grounded in biblical truth. Before our children leave the home, they should be familiar with the basic theological truths presented in the Word, as well as the territories of mystery, and the clear boundaries of heresy. To provide just a few examples of these essentials:

- The doctrines of the Trinity and the Two Natures of Christ (and the mystery of these doctrines)
- The nature of justification and sanctification, and how they relate
- The relationship of God's sovereignty and man's free will (and the mysteries of it)
- The right and wrong uses of the law of God
- The laws of God as laid out for the individual, family, church, and state
- The covenants of the promise, and how the Gentiles have access to these covenants
- The nature of the church as an organic body, an olive tree, a candlestick, and a vine
- The mysteries of the sacraments of Baptism and the Lord's Supper (and how to handle these mysteries with humility and care)
- The work of Christ and what it accomplished
- The work of the Holy Spirit and what it accomplishes
- The problems with the major heretical worldviews of human-

ism, relativism, eastern mysticism, Islam, and cults

5. Teach the whole Word. I recommend reading for distance as well as depth. Our children need to know the entire story of God's covenant people from Old Testament into the New Testament. They should be familiar with the themes in every book of the Bible.

6. Bring other teachers into your home. When I speak of other teachers, I mean the great pastors and teachers with which the Church has been blessed over the last two thousand years (Eph. 4:11). These are gifts to the Church and we all should avail ourselves of them via books or recordings. During family gatherings, we have read books like Augustine's *Confessions*, John Bunyan's *Pilgrim's Progress*, *Grace Abounding to the Chief of Sinners*, *Foxe's Book of Martyrs*, Eusebius' *Ecclesiastical History*, Augustine's *Confessions*, and books written by the Puritans. As a pastor and teacher myself, I have found it useful to listen to sermons from older preachers like D. Martyn Lloyd-Jones as a family. This provides another teacher for my children, and they can watch how I am impacted by these powerful messages from one of the greatest teachers of the 20th Century.

7. Focus on several key books of the Bible. Since it is practically impossible to train our children to be seminary theologians and experts on all 66 books of the Bible in 18 years, there is some wisdom in focusing on several key books.

Focus on the Book of Genesis as providing a framework for history and God's dealings with man. This important book of the Bible sets the Christian perspective apart from the rest of the worldviews in the world in regards to origins, science, sociology, anthropology, history, and redemption.

Focus on the Book of Proverbs as God's Book on Life, specifically designed for training young men and women in knowledge, wisdom, and understanding (Prov. 1:1-6). If we gave our children a great education in everything else, but forgot God's book of wisdom intended for the education of our children, we would be very poor parents indeed.

Focus on the Book of Psalms as God's Book on Worship and Spiritual Battle. It is the very life-blood of the Christian who faces spiritual struggles. Christ had the Psalms on His lips at the cross, and the words of the Psalms should be written on the hearts of our children. They should know the basic content of every one of the 150 psalms by the time they leave the home. This is a tall order, but if we see that God's Word is of higher value than every other book in the world, then we will spend a few hours in it every day.

Focus on at least one Gospel—Matthew, Mark, Luke, or John. Your children should be very familiar with every one of these "periscopes" of the life of our Lord Jesus Christ, the very Son of God who came to save His people from their sins. As far as the teachings of Christ goes, your children should know the content from beginning to end of at least one of the Gospels. These Gospels contain the story of salvation and the revelation of Jesus Christ, the Son of God. If we want our children to know Jesus and to know the Gospel, and to go to heaven, they should be very familiar with this revelation.

Focus on at least one doctrinal epistle. I would recommend Ephesians or Romans. The theology contained in the Bible is not organized in the same way in which systematic theologies are presented. Essential to the Bible's theology are the organic connections made between the smaller components and the whole, which is why the Apostles were constantly mapping out the whole system of redemption in a single paragraph of five to ten verses. Our children should have a comprehensive knowledge of at least one of the epistles, such that they can map out the system of doctrine taught by Peter or Paul.

As a core aspect of the Generations ministry, we have produced in-depth Family Bible Study Guides on these key books of the Bible.

8. Memorize Scripture in order that you might meditate upon it. This is the Psalm 1 lifestyle for the Christian.

> "Blessed is the man who walks not in the counsel of the un-godly, nor stands in the path of sinners, nor sits in the seat of the scornful; but his delight is in the law of the Lord, and in His law he meditates day and night. He shall be like a tree planted by the rivers of water, that brings forth its fruit in its season, whose leaf also shall not wither, and whatever he does shall prosper." (Ps. 1:1-3)

Memorization for the sake of memorization does not do much good, but to memorize so as to saturate oneself in the truths of God's Word is of tremendous value. As we memorize the Word, we are much better prepared to draw it in to our conversations and sweeten our home with God's truth.

A good way to memorize a verse as a family is to recite it three times together. Each family member then takes a turn at it without referring to the text. Should anybody make a mistake, a parent should correct it quickly so that the wrong recitation is not ingrained in everybody's mind. Finally, recite the whole verse again in unison.

9. Pray without ceasing (1 Thess. 5:17). An entire book could be given to the topic of family prayer. This is where we bare our hearts to God and bring out every thanksgiving, every petition, and every praise contained within us. Sometimes, we know there is something that needs to be confessed, and some petition that needs to be drawn out, but we cannot quite verbalize it. Our hearts are heavy, and we know that we are in desperate need of God's help. It is just that we can't quite put a finger on the real issue at hand. In this case, we must rely on the Holy Spirit of God to assist us. We may begin by praying the Word—a verse or a psalm with which we can identify. This is why it is important to know the Psalms and a great deal of the Word.

Provide opportunity for the other members of the household to pray as well. After praying myself, I will offer a long pause so that others may feel free to join in. When it is clear that all have prayed who have felt the need to pray, I will say a final "Amen."

The Christian home should be bathed in prayer, turning to the Lord throughout the day. Even our younger children can be encouraged to pray before meals. Our children should know instinctively where the family goes when there are concerns and anxieties that arise.

Some men find it most difficult to pray out loud with their wives. Could this indicate pride or a lack of sincerity when it comes to their religious faith? We are most forced to honesty when we are with those who know us the best.

I am especially thankful for my mother's prayers. She has been a prayer warrior for many years, and I am convinced that this is one of the chief graces of God that has sustained our family in the faith through the generations. For hours every day, she faithfully prays for her children and her grandchildren. I doubt that there has been an exception to that routine for decades.

Leading by Example

The spiritual temperature of the home is very much dependent upon parents, the spiritual leadership in the family. If we as parents have failed to be moved by the Word of God, how can we expect our children to be impressed by it? Our comfort, our strength, our life, and our joy must come through the Word. When the Word becomes relevant and alive to us, then we have something with which to minister to others in our home.

Of all of the great missionary stories of the 19th Century, the most powerful and inspiring is that of John G. Paton. His autobiography has been greatly influential among Christians over the last 150 years. His faith in the face of the forces of darkness and many threats to his life in the New Hebrides is legendary. His steadfastness to the mission, his love for the people on these islands, and his successes through much adversity, is incomparable to anything you will find in the history of missions. As we read his powerful testimony, we want to know where this man came from. How did he get this vision? We find the answer in the first chapter of his autobiography:

> How much my father's prayers at this time impressed me I can never explain, nor could any stranger understand. When, on his knees and all of us kneeling around him in Family Worship, he poured out his whole soul with tears for the conversion of the Heathen world to the service of Jesus, and for every personal and domestic need, we all felt as if in the presence of the living Savior, and learned to know and love him as our Divine friend. As we rose from our knees, I used to look at the light on my father's face, and wish I were like him in spirit, hoping that, in answer to his prayers, I might be privileged and prepared to carry the blessed gospel to some portion of the heathen world.[25]

There in that rustic home in the highlands of Scotland, an impoverished, simple father (who made his living sewing socks), would gather his nine children around him each day for family worship. The family's priorities were clear, as Paton writes:

> None of us can remember any day ever passed unhallowed thus. No hurry for market, no rush of business, no arrival of friends or guests, no trouble or sorrow, no joy or excitement, ever prevented at least our kneeling around the family altar, while the high priest led our prayers to God, and offered himself and his children there.[26]

In the providence of God, the kingdom of Christ often develops through a multi-generational vision. This takes place whenever the heart of a father for Christ and His Kingdom turns to his son, and his son's heart turns to his father and receives it (Mal. 4:6). When, by the grace of God, fathers pass that vision on to their children through discipleship, the kingdom of God benefits and good things happen. As sons are enabled to stand on the shoulders of their humble fathers, a generational leverage develops for the extension of the Gospel and the further discipleship of the nations. May Christ's kingdom come in our generation by this means!

So. . . what have we learned?

1. What is the "concrete foundation" of a biblical household, and what is the "drywall and carpeting" (using Swanson's analogies)?
2. What are the false gods that the modern household fears?
3. What are some of the ways in which our children see that we fear God?
4. How often should we exhort one another in the Word, according to Hebrews 3:13?
5. What is an exhortation? What is an admonition?
6. What is the main difference between merely reading the Bible and discipleship?
7. What is a good way to develop theological grounding for our children so they are not quickly taken away by cults?
8. Which books of the Bible are recommended for in-depth study to our children by Swanson? Why?
9. Why should we memorize the Word of God?
10. What are the things that should be included in our family prayers?
11. Why do some husbands and wives find it difficult to pray with

each other?

12. How does the example of John G. Paton illustrate the importance of family worship and family discipleship?

So. . . how are we doing?

1. How do you as a parent exemplify the fear of God in your home? Do your children feel secure, or do they feel anxious? How might you be able to grow in this area?

2. How is your home doing when it comes to gratitude? How is gratitude expressed?

3. Rate the following elements of your family devotional life from 0 ("This needs vast improvement"), to 10 ("We're doing well").

- Reading the Bible
- Exhortation
- Catechism
- Scripture Memory
- Psalm and Hymn Singing
- Family Prayer
- Understanding of Genesis
- Understanding of Proverbs
- Understanding of Psalms
- Understanding of a Gospel
- Understanding of an Epistle

4 FAMILY DISCIPLESHIP AND CHARACTER TRAINING

We are not always cognizant of what we really believe. Sometimes what we say we believe and what we really believe are two different things. That's what makes child training such a wonderful thing. There is nothing quite as effective at revealing a parent's worldview, theology, and faith. Speaking of certain teachers and systems of thought, Jesus said, "By their fruits you shall know them." The same thing applies to child training. A bad theology and a bad anthropology will yield bad fruit. Good theology will yield good fruit.

We have seen the fruits of bad child training throughout the years. In 1946, Dr. Benjamin Spock published his famous book *The Common Sense Book of Baby and Child Care*. Popularly considered the expert on parenting, he set the tone for the next three generations with these words "I don't think physical punishment is necessary or particularly effective."[27] The book sold between 50 and 90 million copies. This permissive approach to child training bore its fruit in subsequent years. Among other influential causes, this new humanist psychology contributed a great deal to the breakdown of the character of the nation. Even the mainstream news magazines are calling the millennial generation "the laziest, the unluckiest, the most narcissistic generation" in the history of this country.[28] Through the 1980s and 1990s, fundamentalist Christians then responded with varying approaches that emphasized the importance of the use of the rod and sometimes encouraged a formulaic approach to child-training. That in turn, was followed up by what is now known as "grace-based" child training. In many cases, these various approaches have yielded catastrophic results. Theology and anthropology really do matter. What we believe concerning man's problem, God's law, and God's solution is of the highest importance in the raising of children. Bad theology and bad doctrine form very bad foundations for family life.

Humanism has dominated our institutions for many generations now, which means that most of our schools, universities, churches, and publishing houses do not subscribe to a biblical view of sin, anthropology, and redemption. The humanist assumes that man is born essentially good, and needs only the right education and inputs to optimize his nature and his life. On the other hand, the biblical view describes man as born in sin with an irrepressible inclination to wickedness (Ps. 51:5, Jer. 17:9, Rom. 3:10-12). Reversing this inclination to evil is as impossible as changing a leopard's spots (Jer. 13:23). It is not accomplished by merely adjusting the child's environment or using behavioral modification techniques.

When cruising down a highway, the driver must correct his steering wheel from time to time. This is especially true when the crosswinds exceed 40 mph. Without a constant hand on the steering wheel, the car would quickly be in the ditch. The same principle applies to our understanding and application of doctrine. We are given to imbalance, especially when pride rules our understanding of the basic disciplines in the field of knowledge. Pride gives us a bias for a ditch on the one side or the other of the truth. Those who are concerned mainly with "the other ditch" are most likely sitting in the ditch on the opposite side of the way.

As parents, we must always be open to counsel and correction from others in this serious business of child-rearing. Even as the Word of God is a constant correction to us in our daily walk, so it must be in this area of life.

The remainder of this chapter will outline several important theological and practical balances that we must realize in parenting and character training in our homes.

Authority and Humility

First and foremost, parents must be aware of their God-given authority established by the fifth commandment. Paul repeats the command verbatim in Ephesians 6, but extends the promise to both Jew and Gentile Christians who live on the earth.

> "Honor your father and your mother, that your days may be long upon the land which the Lord your God is giving you." (Ex. 20:12)

This holy commandment is fundamental to Christian parenting. When a police officer pull a motorist over for a traffic violation, rarely would he lose his temper, stomp on the hood of the car, and scream at the motorist. The police officer is calm, cool, and collected, because he understands his authority. He has the backing of the judicial system of the state, the laws of the state, and the constitution of the land. He fulfills his role and realizes the authority that has been invested in him. Similarly, when a young mother pulls her little two year old over for doing 40 mph in a 20 mph zone through the kitchen, she needs to understand her position too. She has been deputized by the Lord of the Universe, and she has been vested with certain authority in her home. It is not absolute authority—only a delegated authority in which she is to receive honor and obedience from her children.

Our Lord Himself took the commandment to honor parents very seriously in Matthew 15 when He condemned the Pharisees for minimizing it by their traditions.

> "He answered and said to them, "Why do you also transgress the commandment of God because of your tradition? For God commanded, saying, 'Honor your father and your mother'; and, 'He who curses father or mother, let him be put to death." (Matt. 15:3-4)

It may come as a shock to some that Jesus would Himself affirm the Old Testament civil sanction of the death penalty for a young man who goes to the extent of cursing his own father or mother. Some have taken great offense to our Lord's position here on the law of God, but we live in an era where antinomianism and rebellion is the rule of the day. Of course, this cursing of father or mother is almost unheard of in societies that still retain some basic social order. Only a society that has witnessed four to five generations of social revolution, political revolution, and cultural revolution would be offended by Jesus' statement in Matthew 15:4.

I was in a grocery store several years ago when I witnessed a young man who was perhaps 16 or 17 years old cursing his father to his face. I remember the feeling of dread that swept over me. It was as if somebody had pulled out a .45 caliber handgun in a public place and began firing into the body of a poor victim. Such crimes are horrific, and in a stable social setting ought to be very rare.

The honoring of parents has very much dissipated in our day, and Christian families should be acutely aware of this. Humans may lose all recognition of God's authority structure, but God does not. He takes His own jurisdictions seriously, more seriously than human civil governments treat their own. We discover God's disposition towards the "teenage" rebel in Proverbs 30:17.

> "The eye that mocks his father, and scorns obedience to his mother, the ravens of the valley will pick it out, and the young eagles will eat it." (Prov. 30:17)

While speaking on child rearing at home education conferences around the country, occasionally I would get the question from a young mother: "My teenage daughter is disobedient, uncooperative, and entirely resistant to my every word. What shall I do?" My first answer invariably would come in the way of a question: "Ma'am, do you fear God?" No doubt, such a response comes as a surprise, but it shouldn't. If the beginning of wisdom is the fear of God in the home, then that applies to parents as much as it does to children. If a parent doesn't fear God and doesn't realize his or her God-given authority on the basis of that reverence, I can't see how a child will learn the fear of God from her parents.

When a parent realizes his authority under God, he must also fear before Him. That sense of authority can turn into an unhealthy authoritarianism, unless it is balanced with due humility before God. As parents, we are just as subject to God as our children are. If we have offended God, we are just as much to humble ourselves, confess our sin, and ask forgiveness. To the extent that sin has a public face, there is need for public confession even in the presence of our children if necessary. When police officers break the law, they should be subject to the same laws to which the rest of the citizens are subject.

Also, parents exemplify their humility and submission when wives submit to their husbands, and when both parents demonstrate due submission to the elders in the church. When fathers break the speed limits and chafe at the civil laws, they should not be surprised when their children resist their authority as well.

Grace and Law

Serious theological differences on the relationship of grace and law, and the relationship of faith and works, have resulted in widely-differing views on child-raising. Many evangelical ministries have separated faith and works, and thereby created a terrible mess for their followers. This is witnessed in the fluctuation between works-less faith and faithless works, in an antinomian and a legalistic outlook often occurring in the same person or ministry. They begin by evangelizing in faith, and then they disciple for works (thereby abandoning faith). The life of works turns into a faithless thing over time, because they see faith as a one-time experience that happened years earlier.

Permissive parents want to emphasize grace without the law, while authoritarian parents emphasize the law over grace. Permissive parents can see only one ditch and that is where the authoritarian legalist lives. However, the legalist will also complain about the permissive parents and their grace-based parenting.

When it comes to the discipleship of our children, the question is sometimes raised: Shall we teach our children to obey before they come to faith in Christ, or shall we see them come to faith in Christ before we teach them to obey the commandments? This is an excellent illustration of the conundrum that faces the evangelical Christian who is confused concerning the relationship of faith and works.

Briefly, here is a summary of the biblical doctrines of faith and works (grace and law).

1. There are three uses of the law, all of which are helpful in the Christian home. The law is a restraining influence to prevent

the non-Christian from being as bad as he could be (1 Tim. 1:9-10, Rom. 13:3-4). The law is a convicting influence that shows our need for Christ (Rom. 3:19, 7:7). And, the law is a rule of obedience for Christians so we may know how to better love God and keep His commandments (John 14:15, Rom. 13:8-9, 1 John 3:22).

2. As Christians, we are not under law as a slave is under a slave master, but we are guided by the law. We are under the reign of grace (Rom. 7:1-4). Our relationship with the law is not one of fear and dread, but is rather like a relationship with a friend.

3. We are justified by grace and through faith alone (Eph. 2:8-9).

4. Faith and works are distinct but not separate in the Christian (Jas. 2:26). "For as the body without the spirit is dead, so faith without works is dead also." We look for true faith and works to come together as a package, and yet they are distinct, as the heads and tails of a coin remain distinct while still part of the same coin.

When we discipline our children with the rod or with verbal rebuke, we are applying the law of God. The speeding ticket does not convey grace, and neither does the rod or the rebuke. As a mother reminds her son that he disobeyed her by touching the hot stove, she presents him with the law. The child is learning more of the law every time he is corrected in any form. We trust that God will effectively use the instruction of the law in our children's lives in various ways. At the very least, the rod may restrain our children from being as bad as they would have been without it. But more than that, we hope that the law will convict them of their sin and show them their need for Christ (Rom. 7:7). After being corrected three hundred times for the same sin, finally we hear our child say the words, "But Daddy, I can't be good!" At this point we gladly tell him, "Yes! I'm so glad you finally realized it, honey. You can't be good! . . . And that is the reason why the Son of God came from heaven to earth. He became man, He was born in a stable in Bethlehem. He was tortured, He suffered and died, and then He rose again. He did all of that, because there is a little boy in our home who can't be good!" The rod cannot save that boy from his sins, and neither can the parent. Only the Lord Jesus Christ can save him from his sins.

The strong-willed child and the special-needs child (or whatever label is used for him) only show more clearly their need for Jesus Christ and His salvation each and every time they disobey their mothers. Even the "impossible," rebellious children repeatedly prove their need for God's grace and the powerful work of Jesus Christ on that cross. Sure, these tough kids will test the faith of their parents, but it is their parents' faith in the power of Christ that gives them the strength and wisdom to deal with these utterly impossible situations. Every time that child sins, the parent should be doubly confident in the power of grace to save him from sin. The child only proves that the parent, the rod, and the corrections cannot save that child from hell without the attendant grace of Jesus Christ. True, the rod plays a part in teaching a child his need for Christ, and to that extent it leads him to the gospel (Prov. 23:14). Consider the following verses, and notice how the law and the use of the rod play an essential part in the discipleship work of parents.

> "For whom the Lord loves He chastens, and scourges every son whom He receives. If you endure chastening, God deals with you as with sons; for what son is there whom a father does not chasten? But if you are without chastening, of which all have become partakers, then you are illegitimate and not sons." (Heb. 12:6-8)

> "He who spares his rod hates his son, but he who loves him disciplines him promptly." (Prov. 13:24)

"Do not withhold correction from a child, for if you beat him with a rod, he will not die. You shall beat him with a rod, and deliver his soul from hell." (Prov. 23:13-14)

"The rod and rebuke give wisdom, but a child left to himself brings shame to his mother." (Prov. 29:15)

The rod, then, is one very important way that our children learn the wisdom contained in the law of God (Ps. 19:7). While the message of the law is helpful, it should not be the dominant force in the home however. The teaching of the law and the rod must come across as a guide, not a slave master. That is why it is so important to regularly bring the gospel of Christ into discussions surrounding discipline. I recommend that every instance of discipline be taken as an opportunity to bring out the gospel. During these moments, we remind our children, "And that's why Jesus Christ came... to save us from our sins. Praise God for this!"

Shall we first teach our children to obey, or do we first teach our children to believe? To teach our children to obey the commandments first will turn them into works-based legalists. To wait until we are sure that they are trusting in Christ before we teach them about the commandments means a parent must never correct a child for his disobedience (and that opposes the instructions of Proverbs 23:13 and many other passages in Scripture). In this case, we would tip into antinomianism. Therefore, we must teach *both* the law of God and the grace of Christ almost in the same breath. If faith and works are distinct but not separate, they ought to be presented as such in the Christian home. We certainly do not want our children getting the impression that self-discipline, the rod, and verbal correction will be sufficient to save them from their sins. If anything, these things will only demonstrate to them the hopelessness of their condition (or it will turn them into hypocrites and legalists). They need a Savior, and that Savior is the Lord Jesus Christ.

Heart and Hands

This third theological balance in the training of children illustrates the way the American religion has gone since the 19th century. When we find the country's highest pornography download rates in those states with the highest church attendance rates (Utah and Mississippi), we come to better understand the powerlessness of American religion.[29] This religion is adept at producing good manners and a well-polished outward appearance, but on the inside we find it is nothing but rotting flesh and dead men's bones (Matt. 23:27). It is a religion that produces a form of godliness, but denies the power thereof (2 Tim. 3:5), which is a key feature of many cults. Until Americans repent of this powerless religion and return to the biblical gospel and biblical churches, we must conclude that much of this branch of modern Christianity is only fit to be burned.

For example, let's say a young mother attends a family conference and for the first time in her life hears a message on modesty. Of course, modesty is important since we do find the principle in Scripture (1 Pet. 3:4, 1 Tim. 2:9), and there aren't many clothing designers offering the "modest line" for the new summer rollout these days. When this mother hears the message she quickly responds by employing a new standard in her home. She decks her girls out in modest dresses, and a few days later they head down to the mall where they come upon a group of young teenage girls who apparently did not get "the memo." The mother points them out to her daughters and says, "Look at those girls strutting their stuff! Now, I am so happy you girls are dressed modestly!" If we were to freeze the scene here, we would find a more fundamental problem developing in this family. The word for modesty used in 1 Timothy 2:9 speaks of "shame," which connotes humility. Now, this mother is cultivating a bigger problem in her daughters. While she was attempting to bring about a form of humility on the outside by comparing her daughters with all of those "immodest natives," she rather inspired a *lack* of humility in her daughters' hearts.

As Christian parents, we are vitally interested in the condition of our children's hearts. We do not want to be externalists or superficial flakes in our parenting. Where there is no fundamental change of heart, we know that all external appearances are only temporary, and vain. A good set of questions to ask yourself when you are conflicted about a particular problem such as dress or music choice with your teen is: "What do I really want out of this child? Am I interested only in a change of clothes? Is that all I am really after? Or do I want a change of heart? Do I want my child to love God with heart, soul, mind, and strength?" Your true desires are a good reflection of your own heart in the matter. If all you want is a certain external compliance to a set of rules, then that does say something about the state of your heart. The answers to the above questions will direct your manner of parenting.

An over-emphasis on externals will usually lead to a narrow application of a broad principle. As I've mentioned before, Christian child-raising gurus proliferated across the landscape offering their individual sets of formulas and recipes over the last thirty years. One particular approach encouraged "timed feedings" for babies. Instead of waiting for the child to "demand" a feeding, the parents would set the schedule. This provided a means by which children could learn respect, submission, and obedience. Books recommending this approach have marketed to millions of parents since the early 1990s. There is now a firestorm of controversy between those who advocate "timed feedings" and those who oppose that particular regimen. Sadly, these sorts of issues have formed unnecessary breaches sometimes within church communities as well.

Of course, you would have to look long and hard to find references to "timed feedings" in the Bible. We would therefore place this sort of advice under the category of "helpful suggestions," in which the child training guru lays out one possible application of a biblical principle. There ought to be a great measure of Christian liberty in these areas, especially where every family's circumstances vary greatly. For some families, incorporating the general rule of timed-feedings for a particular child may work very well. There may be some benefit in teaching a child at least some external compliance to the fifth commandment ("Honor your father and mother.") It is only when the application begins to displace the principle in the minds of those who use it, that things go wrong. This is just one more form of legalism and autonomy where man becomes a law to himself. The application begins to take on more authority than the original principle laid down in the Word under the authority of the Holy Spirit of God.

There are many ways to apply and to teach the fifth commandment in our homes. It is when we narrow the application to the one that seems best to us, and implicitly or explicitly impose it on others that problems arise. This imposition can happen through our attitudes, or the books and sermons we share, or the conversations that take place in the foyer of the church. Sometimes, quite inadvertently we find ourselves abridging the Christian liberty of others and undermining the original principle found in God's Word.

Once more, the reader should observe both ditches next to this path. To narrow the application to one particular form, in the end marginalizes the authority of the principle. This is legalism and another form of autonomy. The other ditch, however, is just as dangerous because it ignores the principle altogether and refuses to make any application at all. This is antinomianism.

Consider the most basic principle for the education of a child — Proverbs 1:7. The fear of the Lord is the fundamental basis of knowledge. Some have found that home education provides one good context in which we may teach the fear of God as the epistemological basis of knowledge. However, there are parents who declare homes-chooling to be the only possible application for this principle in the education of a child. I like to point out to homeschooling parents the story of a family who took an entire year to ride bicycles across America. I'm sure some homeschooler might point out that these folks had abandoned God's plan for their children when they chose to "bike school" instead of "homeschooling!" Undoubtedly, this family could have educated their children very well in many sundry ways in the fear and reverence of God as they witnessed God's creation across the fruited plains. God's Word allows a great deal of latitude and liberty in the education of our children, even more so than the current political state would allow. It is when we reduce the principle to our favorite application that we will lose sight of the principle itself. Many homeschooling families actually fail to teach their children in the fear of God, whereas there are Christian schools and public schools with Christian teachers may ver well do a better job fulfilling the biblical principle over the years.

Those Christians who tend to focus more upon the external elements of the Sabbath principle (the fourth commandment), modesty for women, certain restrictions on music in worship, manners of conduct, or habits of diligence in the home, will eventually betray a lack of genuine faith and love. They obsess on the externals as the Pharisees did in the time of Christ. While we would not want to dismiss the importance of the Sabbath principle, modesty, psalmody, manners, or tithing (Matt. 23:23), the heart of the matter remains the heart of the matter. Straining at gnats and swallowing camels means that the Pharisees tend to ignore the camels (Matt. 23:24). It is faith, judgment, and mercy that are of first importance in our lives and in the life of the family.

True, parents have less control of their children's hearts than their children's external behavior, but we should at least seek to discern the heart in every issue, and speak to heart issues. We can show our concern for the heart of the matter when speaking to our children, and this itself becomes the most important contribution any Christian parent can give to the discipleship of their children. Healthy, loving relationships are essential in this discerning process, so that we may speak more specifically to heart matters in the individual lives of each of our children.

Rules and Relationships

This fourth balance introduces yet another major battle that rages within evangelical Christianity today—rules vs. relationships. Churches advertise their programs, loudly declaring they are about relationships, not rules. The most popular Christian book of the last decade fell hard into this ditch. William Paul Young writes as though God were speaking: "The Bible doesn't teach you to follow rules. . . Just don't look for rules and principles; look for relationship—a way of coming to be with us."[30] Then, there were some child-training systems produced by fundamentalist groups in the 20th century which seemed to be primarily about enforcing rules, and little was said about relationships. Once again, the blind lead the blind and they both fall into the ditch on one side or the other. There ought not to be a preference for rules over relationship, or relationship over rules. The Bible affirms both rules and relationship as fundamental to the Christian life.

In the final judgment, Jesus Christ proclaims to the goats, "I never knew you [had a relationship with you]; depart from Me, you who practice lawlessness [those who oppose God's rules]!" (Matt. 7:23b). Clearly, the Old and New Testaments affirm many times over that God wants us to "love Me and keep My commandments" (Deut. 5:10, Deut. 7:9, Deut. 11:1, Neh. 1:5, Dan. 9:4, John 14:15, 1 John 5:3, 2 John 1:6). It is hard to miss the point: the Lord wants us both loving Him and keeping His commandments. Only the grossest form of heresy would separate these two fundamental elements of the Christian faith. Sadly, this heresy has infected too much of the Christian faith, confusing millions, if not hundreds of millions of professing believers. These two elements that describe the true believer are crucial in the final analysis — because these will be the criteria by which the believer is described in the day of final judgment. None of this should be taken to infer that we are justified by works, or that we are saved by our own merits, or that we need to live sinless, perfect lives. Keeping God's commandments refers to a respect for the commandments of God, even a love of God's laws (Rom. 7:22, Ps. 119:97).

The Pharisees refused to realize their misuse of the law of God, according to Jesus, because their hearts were far from God (Matt. 15:6-8). Their failure to keep the law of God and their disrespect for the law of God originated from hearts that were in rebellion against God. Thus, Christian parents must act out of hearts that love God and reverence His commandments. As well, we should desire that our children will love God *and* keep His commandments.

On a Sunday afternoon, a mother instructs her young son not to play in the front yard in his good clothes. Later in the day, she is dismayed to see him still in his Sunday best, swimming in the neighbor's pool. Calling him out of the pool, she proceeds to chide him for his disobedience. However, the boy plays the lawyer and points out that she had failed to specify the neighbor's backyard pool in her original instructions. Her response is no different than how Jesus responded in Matthew 15:8. She tells the boy, "You must not love me, son, because if you had loved me you would have known that I didn't want you playing in the neighbor's pool in your Sunday clothes."

There is a necessary affinity between rules and relationship, in that the relationship does not require a great deal of specification, court proceedings, negotiations, and argument. In fact, the New

Testament provides far less specification when it comes to the laws relating to "taste not, touch not, and handle not" (Col. 2:21). These external rules produced a religion described by New Testament authors as "the rudiments of the world" (Col. 2:8, Gal. 4:3). While love transcends a rule-oriented existence in home and life in general, this does not completely eliminate all laws from the Christian experience. We still need a concrete sense of what pleases God and what does not please God, and this we find in the Ten Commandments, the Beatitudes, Ephesians 5, and elsewhere throughout Scripture. However, the application of God's laws in the daily routines of life really does require a love for Him with heart, mind, and strength.

When our children are younger, we choose their clothing, their food, and the books they read. As they grow older, we do not want to love God with all of our minds and our souls *for them*. We want them to love God with all of their minds, so that they will learn to make their own godly choices with clothing, food, and entertainment. Ideally, this transition should be completed by the end of the teen years. Of course, we hope that they will seek counsel from their parents and other mature adults in the church body as well.

Occasionally, a young father will ask me how long a little toddler with ants in his pants should be able sit still during family devotions. I like to point out that the Bible has nothing to say directly about this, especially if the boy has ants in his pants. So there is no way that I can answer this question for them. Training a young boy with ants in his pants isn't something that can be done by using a rigid set of rules issued by some expert a thousand miles away who is writing a book on child discipline. How long should a little boy sit still during Bible time? That depends on how long he was able sit still yesterday, and how many ants are in his pants today. It depends on how much you love him and how much he loves you. It depends on a lot of things, but mostly it depends on relationship. Indeed, it is impossible to raise children in the Christian home without a profound appreciation for and cultivation of relationship.

Sovereignty and Human Responsibility

What does a father do when his child responds to discipline with, "Daddy, I don't want to be good!"? This is when the parent realizes his absolute reliance upon the sovereign grace of God to bring about salvation in this child's life.

When running the Indy-500, the Christian race car driver isn't going to "leave it all up to the sovereignty of God." He should know that the whole disposing of the race is in the hands of God (Prov. 16:33), but he is still imminently sensible of his own responsibility. The race-car driver checks his tire pressure, he checks his engine compression, and he runs a few practice laps. He does everything within his abilities to maximize the possibilities of his success in the race. God predestines the means as well as the ends. He predestines that there are faithful men who take up their responsibilities seriously in order that they may win the race. No less than this, Christian parents should apply themselves to the work of raising their children with all diligence, consistency, passion, interest, prayer, and teaching in the Word. It is for lack of visionary, faithful, humble fathers, and diligent, sacrificial, loving, and faithful mothers that children are not raised in the nurture and the admonition of the Lord.

Yet, at the very same time, we must be trusting in a sovereign, powerful, gracious, and loving God who will work in us both to will and to do of His good pleasure. We stand in the grace of God, and believe in the sovereign power of God, while we do the work of the kingdom of God.

Other Aspects of Good Balance in the Christian Home

The following may be seen as a derivative of the theological balances previously considered, because theological balance should always work its way out practically. We need for example, a good balance of affection and correction. The absence of affirmation is a good sign that there is not much love and grace in the home, and an unhealthy bent towards law and rules. Our children's lives should be surrounded with affirmation, attended by a little correction showing up here and there throughout the day. Affirmation is only an effect of gratefulness to God for His every gift evident in the lives of others. Grateful homes are affirming homes.

Persistence and Promptitude

The Scripture does not give us a great deal of specific advice on the raising of children, however there is important wisdom to be gleaned. We ought to carefully consider what is given to us. Two adverbs are used in two key passages that demand our attention.

> "You shall teach them *diligently* to your children, and shall talk of them when you sit in your house, when you walk by the way, when you lie down, and when you rise up." (Deut. 6:7)

> "He who spares his rod hates his son, but he who loves him disciplines him *promptly*." (Prov. 13:24)

These two words, "diligently" and "promptly," offer important insight into the way children are to be raised in the properly-balanced Christian home. Teaching diligently conveys the idea of repetition and consistency over a long period of time.

A certain Christian teaching that became popular over previous generations was the matter of "breaking the will." We were told that the parent should discipline until he or she "breaks the will of the child." Such teaching was rooted in the wrong view of the child's nature. It was assumed that the child was more like a horse that could be trained to obey by behavioral modification. With enough discipline, as the thinking goes, a child could be trained to obey any rule and to achieve any standard. Of course, the fruit of such thinking is a temporary, external obedience. These children learned a few good manners and they could say, "Yes sir," and "No sir," but they were only whitened tombs. When the external crust finally cracked wide open, green goo poured everywhere. It was not long before everybody knew that this was just one more example of an external religion lacking the power to really accomplish anything significant.

Rather than commanding a father to "break the will" when he disciplines, the Bible provides the command to teach diligently and consistently for a very long time. The Hebrew word used is "shinantam," which is derived from the idea of sharpening a sword. As parents and disciplers, we are called to plant the seeds and water the plants. The fruit is in God's hands. We have no idea precisely when the plants are regenerated.

As parents, we should avoid the two ditches of presumption and faithlessness. On the one hand, we may be too presumptuous and assume that all is fine because a child was baptized or because he tossed a pinecone into the fire at summer camp and gave his life to Jesus on July 14, 2013. Or we may be too faithless, and assume that the Spirit of God has never worked and will never work in our child's life. We do not expect to win the race in a day. We must be faithful farmers. We baptize our children and we teach them, because these are the two things we are called to do in the Great Commission. After 18-20 years of discipleship, we will have seen good weeks and bad weeks, good years and bad years. By God's grace, we will see fruit when they begin to disciple their friends for Jesus, or when they begin the process over again with their own children.

We do not expect our children's external and internal behavior (hands and heart) to change entirely overnight. To pretend that it will or to attempt to achieve it by pure force is the way to create little hypocrites. Expecting children to immediately conform to perfection in this way exalts the sovereignty of man over the sovereignty of God. Regeneration, in the Parable of the Sower, must happen somewhere between planting the seed and identifying the fruit (Matt. 13:1-23). We don't have an x-ray machine that can examine the heart under the soil, so it is impossible to know how and where and when the Holy Spirit is working. I encourage parents to be good farmers and expect a crop in twenty years. Don't give up; just consistently do the Deuteronomy 6:7 work day in and day out, year in and year out.

The second key word is translated "promptly" in the New King James Version of Proverbs 13:24. Given our long-term perspective of child training, there may be a temptation to be slack at various points along the way. Patience does not imply inattentiveness and inaction. Again, if we picture the garden analogy, we are encouraged to watch for weeds. This is moment-by-moment discipline. The farmer walks his field each morning, waiting for the next weed to pop up, and he pulls it promptly. Of course, he understands that this will not be the last sign of weeds in the garden, but he stays on his game.

There is that tendency for parents to let disobedience, disrespect, complaining, and ingratitude slip into the home. Take for example, the home where there has been almost no discipline for complaining over a period of months. The problem begins to snowball. In such cases, I would encourage parents to repent before their children for their slackness in discipline and then get back into the game. Before the day starts, Dad should explain to the children the egregiousness of the sin of ingratitude and the need for confession of sin. He asks each member of the family to mention something for which they are grateful, and then they all get on their knees together and lift up prayers of thanksgiving. Then, Dad explains to the children that from here on out they will be watching for signs of complaining and both parents will discipline for it. On the very first sign of whining, a parent immediately addresses it with firm correction. This will usually awaken the home to the seriousness of the problem. Throughout the day, Dad and Mom should stay consistent with some form of correction when the problem arises, and the following day, and so on.

When parents issue temporary or permanent rules in the home, they should enforce these rules consistently (I don't recommend that they issue too many rules). When parents let things slip without a faithful word of admonition and rebuke, or proper corporeal discipline, sins will begin to compound in the home. To allow disobedience, disrespect, or the abuse of God's name to predominate in the home is to give place to lies and deceit. When a child sins, he promotes the lie that sin is permitted. Before God, every parent has a duty to correct these sins by his own confessions, and by admonitions, warnings, and rebukes.

Most older, experienced parents recommend that correction begin early in a child's life. They will tell you that children generally understand more than you think they do, when it comes to correction. Again, this correction may very well be a simple admonition or a rebuke, as in, "No!"

Structure and Freedom

There is much to be said about the balance of structure and freedom within the home, but once again, theology is critical to a right understanding and application. As Christians, we are Trinitarian, meaning that the Christian view of reality is defined by both the oneness and the "manyness" of God. In the pattern of God's creation we discover both order (the one) and messiness (the many). We steadfastly refuse to err on one side or the other. Overly-scheduled homes and overly-clean homes strike us as a bit "Unitarian." Modern schools and large monolithic institutions require a great deal of structure in order to operate efficiently. These conditions have formed out of Unitarian statism over the last century or two. When the nation turned away from Trinitarianism in the universities and the political systems, this very much affected the structure and form of education and child training. On the other hand, overly-messy homes and unscheduled lives indicate a bit of "polytheism." In a biblical, Trinitarian home, there will develop a better balance between structure and freedom, schedules and spontaneity, order and functionality. And, every home situation is unique for each Christian family. All are subject to the same principles in the Word of God, but there are vast differences in how these principles are employed across the many family situations!

In conclusion, it should be clear by now that a right theology will produce a right balance in the Christian family and in human society as well. I sincerely hope that these guidelines will serve as "reflective road markers" on the "road of life" to help the Christian family navigate without careening into the ditch on the left or the right. By now, we as parents should have a better sense for the "impossibility" of getting it exactly right. This is way above our skill level, our natural wisdom and ability. Nobody captures it perfectly. We must make course corrections in our thinking, our theological meanderings, and our practice along the way. We must stay humble and stay on our knees. It is only by the grace of God that we make it.

Postscript

Based on my observations as a leader in the church for 25 years, here are the qualities of the families that "make it." They face their crises like everybody else, but by the grace of God they make it.

1. They are humble, and proactively seek counsel from the elders in the church about their marriage troubles before things get too out of hand.

2. They are humble, and when they run into troubles with their teenaged children they seek counsel from the elders in the

church. These parents will openly confess their own sins first, before their children are offered the opportunity to confess their sins.

3. They are humble, and they assume that other parents are doing a better job than they are. Even if they believe they have found a better method for educating their children, they will assume that another Christian family (who avails themselves to more secular forms) is doing better in aggregate than they are.

4. They are humble, and they weep over their own sins in front of their children.

5. They are humble, and they are willing to sacrifice fame and fortune in favor of their relationships.

6. They are humble, and they serve the widows, the orphans, and the generally-neglected poor in the church body (with no expectation for reward).

7. They are humble, and they are the first to confess sins in any conflict (and they don't confess their sins in order to prime the pump for others to confess theirs).

8. They are humble, and they utterly depend on God's grace for their children. This manifests itself in constant prayer. They take no confidence in recipes and formulas.

9. They are humble, and they seldom or never raise accusations against anybody else in the church body. They bear criticism without gossiping or retribution. They assume the best of others, and refuse to judge people based upon externals.

10. They are humble, and they do not have the mentality that "no church is good enough for us." They are not church-hoppers.

I trust my reader sees a pattern in the above list. Many "Christian" families start out looking quite promising, but after twenty years there is to be found a steady stream of broken relationships in their wake, along with bitterness, wrecked marriages, fornication, incest, general apostasy, mental struggles, drug problems, or even criminal activity. If you were to identify one universal, fundamental flaw in those families, it is pride.

> "But He gives more grace. Therefore He says: 'God resists the proud, But gives grace to the humble.'" (Jas. 4:6)

So. . . what have we learned?

1. How does driving a car down a windblown highway compare to raising children?
2. What are the fruits of a permissive society? How does a humanist worldview produce a permissive approach to child rearing?
3. What is the difference between the Old Testament and New Testament handling of the fifth commandment?
4. How does Jesus Christ treat the fifth commandment?
5. How does a parent's fear of God produce a right perspective concerning parental authority in the minds of both the parent and the child?
6. How does a father exemplify humility? How does a mother exemplify humility?
7. What are the three uses of the law? How are these used in training our children?
8. What is the relationship of faith and works as described in James 2:24?
9. Should we teach our children to obey before we teach them to believe in Christ? Or is it the other way around? Explain.
10. According to Jesus in Matthew 15:1-8, what were the two concerns He had with the Pharisees? What are the two things that Jesus will bring up in the final judgment (see Matthew 7:23)?
11. What are some of the indications that Christians or Christian

parents are focused more on externals and less on the heart?

12. Describe the two ditches of antinomianism and legalism as we seek to apply the principles of God's Word.

13. How does the Parable of the Sower help us to understand the parent's role in the discipleship of children?

14. How would we know if a parent was veering into the ditch of faithlessness on one hand or presumption on the other?

15. Why are relationships important for children who must learn to honor and obey their parents, as illustrated with the little boy who jumped in the neighbor's pool dressed in his Sunday best?

16. What does the Bible say about rules and relationships? Does it favor one over the other?

17. What are the two key adverbs found in the Bible which provide a framework for raising our children?

18. How does the doctrine of the Trinity affect the way you run your home?

So... how are we doing?

1. How do you handle applications like "timed feedings" or "homeschooling?" Do you properly distinguish principle from application?

2. Towards which ditch might your family tend to err, if one or the other element is ignored of the following pairs?

a. Recognizing Your Authority - Maintaining Humility

b. Grace - Law

c. Rules - Relationship

d. Heart - Hands

e. Reliance on God's Sovereignty - Human Responsibility

f. Affection - Correction

g. Persistence - Promptitude

h. Structure - Freedom

5 THE FAMILY ECONOMY

Vast changes came over social systems throughout the entire world between 1960 and the present day. The disintegrated family followed upon the toxic combination of the sexual revolution, the decimated family economy, and a dominant feminist ideology. Betty Friedan, who authored the landmark book, *The Feminine Mystique* in 1963, best captured the feminist socio-economic vision with the memorable words, "It is better for a woman to compete impersonally in society, as men do, than to compete for dominance in her own home with her husband, compete with her neighbors for empty status, and so smother her son that he cannot compete at all." Of equal influence, feminist-writer Gloria Steinem also wrote, "A liberated woman is one who has sex before marriage and a job after."

By all indicators, the family has mostly disintegrated as a meaningful socioeconomic unit in the 21st century. The nuclear family now makes up less than half of American households, for the first time in history. Half of children born to millennial women are born outside of wedlock (up from 6% in 1960),[31][32] and the shack-up rate is ten times what it was in 1970. The divorce rate is ten times what it was in 1880,[33] and the average marriage age for young men and women continues to rise. The problem is bound to get much worse with the millennial generation, give that three-quarters of them support homosexual marriage.[34] A full 75% of women from 25 to 54 years of age are sent out of their homes into the workforce every day, up from 20% in 1900.[35] These trends represent exactly the vision of the feminists that took the world by storm over the last sixty years.

The resultant birth implosions worry economists.[36] Japan, America, and the European Union face soaring debt-to-GDP ratios as their populations age and their birth rates continue to sag. It is a socio-economic disaster waiting to happen.

While women are taking the jobs, men are increasingly leaving the workforce. Even the secular media points to the "end of men" and the "demise of guys."[37] In a recent article from Newsweek Magazine, we read that 70% of men have not reached maturity by 30 years of age (based on metrics like holding down a job and raising a family), up from 30% in 1960.[38] The median income for young men under 30 years of age has taken a nosedive since 1970, the only demographic to have taken such a hit.

All of this points to a steady and concerted abandonment of God's plan for the family, and His withdrawal of common grace at the most basic level of human society. In the past, God preserved the family even in pagan countries, but that can no longer be said for the Western world where the family is dying a slow and miserable death. Almost every major institution, whether political, educational, economic, cultural, or medical, is organized so as to marginalize and deconstruct the family as a viable social unit.

Serious Christians are looking for something that will restore the family unit in the present day. It hardly seems realistic that the nuclear family will be salvaged by an occasional family game night or a once-a-week reunion at a restaurant somewhere in the city. We trust that God has something else in mind for the Christian family wherever it still exists.

The Words of Jesus Christ Concerning the Human Family

The words of Jesus speak authoritatively and most directly to the present milieu. In reference to the institution of marriage, He says,

> "The two shall become one flesh. . . . they are no longer two but one flesh. therefore, what God has joined together, let not man separate." (Matt.19:5b-6)

This is the ideological basis for the unity of the family, and every defense of the family unit must include this authoritative word. When Jesus offered the ominous warning, "Let not man separate," certainly He must have been aware of the powerful institutional forces that have worked hard to destroy family unity. In our century, we are not concerned merely with the easy divorce laws and the arguments between husbands and wives in the kitchen. Every tax code, every political institution, every college class, and every economic system that has ordered the segregation of the family unit over the last 250 years must assume some responsibility for the wholesale dismantling of this God-ordained institution in the Western world.

Churches have also failed to defend the biblical doctrine of the family by their theology of pure individuation (ignoring the covenantal themes in Scripture). The Bible speaks of the solidarity of the household unit in Old Testament and New Testament alike. Any attempt to find a different treatment of family in the New Testament vs. the Old Testament is a pure fabrication. We find families in the New Testament serving God together (Stephanas), believing together (Cornelius), being baptized together (Lydia, the Philippian jailer, Stephanas, and Cornelius), and working together (Aquila and Priscilla). The disintegration of family unity has led to the gradual erosion of generational continuity in the faith over the last two hundred years as well.

Economic Retrograde

Economic forces have also devastated family integrity. In the opening paragraphs of his famous autobiography, written in 1888, the missionary John G. Paton lamented the destruction of the family farm and the family economy in Scotland, and he said "the loss to the nation as a whole [was] vital, if not irreparable."[39]

When fathers and mothers left their homes for corporate jobs, their children were initially turned over to the capitalist corporation. Subsequently, the children were then passed off to the state by way of child labor laws and compulsory attendance laws. A hundred years later, the same thing is happening to the women who moved from their homes to the corporation in search of security and benefits. Recently, medical insurance coverage shifted towards the state by way of Obamacare. Some have estimated the recent Obamacare marriage penalty to be as high as $11,000 per year.[40]

In the political sphere, members of the home were set against each other in the voting booth. The strongest, most-identifiable socialist voting base that led to the election of Barack Obama in 2008 and 2012 was single women.[41] Where there is no family to provide "social" security, the socialist state does the honors. As long as the majority of households are led by single women, and the nuclear family makes up less than half of American households, we will never see a reprieve in the rise in big government. Western governments will continue to expand until the economies collapse—unless God sends a religious, social, cultural, and moral reformation.

As far back as the 1920s, Hilaire Belloc and G.K. Chesterton warned that capitalism and communism represented inherently unstable social systems that would undermine the family and self-destruct. They argued for a "third way" family-based economy with a widespread ownership of property (debt-free) that would protect "primal family relations and the home economy." They warned that "measures such as unemployment insurance, a minimum wage, and national health insurance constituted a dangerous new form of servitude." [42]

All of the above factors have worked in concert to break down the unity of biblical marriage and the household economy in most Western nations, and now the developing nations as well. By far the strongest of the external forces that have worked to separate the oneness of the family is the modern economic-educational cartel.

The Definition of the Family Economy

The family economy is formed when a man marries a woman, and she serves as his helper in the dominion task (Gen. 2:18). An ax head by itself is of little use to take down trees. Place an ax head on an ax handle, and the capability for useful work has increased a hundred fold. This illustrates the basic elements of the family economy as designed by God.

The 31st chapter of Proverbs presents a picture of the wife's role in the family economy. It is entirely foreign to the current socio-economic scenario, so most of the world would reject the wisdom contained in this chapter. However, a more careful study reveals something more stable, more solid, more beneficial, more lasting, and more fulfilling than the vision of Betty Friedan or Gloria Steinem.

> "Who can find a virtuous wife? For her worth is far above rubies. The heart of her husband safely trusts her; so he will have no lack of gain. She does him good and not evil all the days of her life." (Prov. 31:10-12)

We do not read here that, "The heart of her corporate boss and seven layers of bureaucracy safely trust in her." Rather, "the heart of her husband safely trusts in her, so he will have no lack of gain." Scripture assumes the family economy, and the wife plays a crucial role in it.

When unbelievers like Betty Friedan are concerned that a wife would need to "compete for dominance in her own home with her husband," she has entirely missed the biblical vision for the marriage and the household. She assumes that there is no complementation between husband and wife, there is no mutual appreciation for each other, and there is no love in that household. In Friedan's egalitarian view of economic struggle between genders and classes, she sees nothing but a dog-eat-dog competition between husband and wife. She assumes there will be no family economy operating. She assumes that mothers will be smothering their sons because there are no fathers and male mentors to disciple young men into their work. These are two radically different social systems, one formed by the modern feminist and the other laid down by God.

Traveling through an airport in Chicago several years ago, I recall seeing large posters picturing an African woman that read, "The World's Most Untapped Natural Resource." *What a degrading, dehumanizing depiction of a woman!* I thought to myself. When large governments and corporations working in collusion to seek out the last few free women left in the world for their own use, I think we have lost any sense of the dignity of the Proverbs 31 woman forever.

The prophet Samuel warned that powerful kings would take a tenth of the daughters to become "perfumers, cooks, and bakers" in 1 Samuel 8:13, but he considered this to be an intolerable tyranny. Similarly, Nehemiah was concerned about the dissolution of household economies in his day (Neh. 5:5).

The family economy is so fundamental to a biblical view of life that it is mentioned in the Fourth Commandment. It is assumed that our sons and daughters make up an important part of the family economy for six days out of the week.

> "Remember the Sabbath day, to keep it holy. Six days you shall labor and do all your work, but the seventh day is the Sabbath of the Lord your God. In it you shall do no work: you, nor your son, nor your daughter, nor your male servant, nor your female servant, nor your cattle, nor your stranger who is within your gates." (Ex. 20:8-10)

An understanding of the family economy is basic to family life, but it is largely missing from the modern mind. How many times do you hear people speak of "our family economy?" Right away, there are many misconceptions that arise when speaking of family economy. This is not the "traditional" family where the father works and the mother stays home; nor is it the latchkey family where children are raised by the state to play their part in the statist economy. It is an *oikonomia*, which is the Greek word from which our English word, "economics" is taken. The Greek word *oikonomia*, is translated as "family law" or "household law." The basic economic unit is not an individual and it is not a corporation or the government. According to the creation mandate and 5,900 years of historical practice, the basic economic unit is the family. If this brief summary could only revive the concept and the terminology of the family economy for a few Christian families, that would be a great step in the renewal of the family itself in the modern day.

Simply defined, the family economy is comprised of everything that a family does in seven twenty-four hour days every week. It subsumes every ministry effort, every instance of hospitality, every act of service, every chore, every contract job, every entrepreneurial endeavor, and every corporate task (as an employee) that the members of the family execute. Technically, every family has a family economy. When a family does not recognize their family economy, the usual result is a gradual fragmentation of the family itself, year by year, and generation by generation.

When people ask if we are a one-income family or a two-income family, I like to tell them that we are a "seven-income" family. Our family economy is also identified by more than our quid-pro-quo economic endeavors. Our family is involved in hospitality (every week), visitation of the elderly and the sick (every week), pro-life sidewalk counseling, dog breeding, missions trips to orphanages around the world, discipleship and mentorship, radio broadcasts, and a hundred other things.

For 5,900 years, families worked together: David was feeding his father's sheep, Rachel was feeding her father's sheep, Joseph was feeding his father's sheep, and Aquila and Priscilla worked together as tentmakers. When a young man would leave his family's economy, he would cleave to his wife and form another family economy (Matt. 19:5).

If a father works a corporate job, he provides one income stream for the family economy, but that should not be the sum total of it. If that is the view of the average family today, the family economy is barely operable. Children are seldom seen as part of the family economy. For several generations, educational systems have increasingly removed children from the family and the family economy and placed them into a socialist economy. Mothers are seldom seen as the business manager of the household economy. While entrepreneurism and family businesses must not be considered the extent of the family economy, the rarity of such activity indicates the slow but steady death of family economics.

The Challenges Facing the Family Economy

Following the Industrial Revolution and the family-fragmenting economies of the last six generations, the family economy has taken some big hits. Households are saddled with twenty times the debt slavery that they were in 1900 (adjusted for inflation), seven times more government control and taxation (as a percentage of the GNI), and about five times more corporate servitude.[43] Increasing levels of servitude like this make it more and more difficult to form healthy family economies. When children are plugged into the state as early as their preschool or kindergarten years, the importance of the family and the family economy dissipates early on in their minds. As they wander away from their families into an increasingly socialist world, they face ever-decreasing odds that they will ever launch a family of their own.

An average millennial (we'll call him David) enrolls in college two thousand miles from home, gets an apartment, and plays computer games until he's 29. David hooks up with Rachel for three months, dumps her, and thinks about having kids when he's 48. He gets his first job nailed down at 30 and pays off his college debts at 38. Meanwhile, Rachel goes off to college, gets her career going, freezes her eggs, tries not to get pregnant, but decides she may have one or two children before she's 45 years old (whether or not she is married). She doesn't really need a husband, as long as socialist programs and corporate benefits will take care of her in her waning years. This is not the life of the average Baby Boomer from the 1960s, or the life of the Silent Generation of the 1940s. It is the life of the millennial, the death of the nuclear family, and the eventual failure of a socio-economic system. As both social and economic systems are bound to fail, it is time to turn to the implementation of the biblical socio-economic approach. God's ways of family and economy are always better and sure to be fruitful in re-establishing a healthy civilization in the years to come.

The education and discipleship of the children are important elements of the family economy that must be integrated into it. However, these must never be considered the sum total of the family economy. They are only subsidiary parts of it. Education prepares our children to become even more effective in economic and ministry work.

One of the reasons why young men are in the shape they are in—playing computer games at 34 years of age, and the only demographic making less money than they did in 1970—is that they were not trained to work when they were young boys. For the last three generations, young men have not been mentored by their fathers. "School," as traditionally configured, does not train a boy to work. It is a grave error to wait until a boy is 16 or 18 years old before he is put to work, and millions of young millennials are suffering for it.

A humanist-socialist system that promises womb-to-tomb security undermines family responsibilities and relationships and destroys the character of the next generation. A society like this cannot survive. As England's prime minister Margaret Thatcher put it, "the problem with socialism is that eventually you will run out of other people's money." After having eliminated eighty million babies by abortion and the abortifacient pill, America now faces a birth implosion where the worker-to-retiree ratio will be one third of what it was in 1950 twenty years hence. With the burgeoning debt and eighty million retiring baby boomers, America, not to mention all the other socialist nations, will learn Thatcher's lesson well. What happens to a society in which the 30-year-old guys are playing computer games while the 65-year-old baby boomers are playing golf? These socialist systems will not survive, and the only reasonable solution will be healthy family economies. The economic situation is dire. Unless we change the way we educate, the way we do our economics, and the way we conduct family life, I tremble to think of what will happen in the upcoming decades. Now is the time to redefine a biblical economy based upon the re-integration of the human family.

The Benefits of the Family Economy

Fathers and mothers must train their sons and daughters to contribute to the household economy from the early years. Meanwhile, parents need to be thinking of laying up an inheritance for their children (2 Cor. 12:14, Prov. 13:22), and their children will take care of them in their old age. These are the three legs on the stool of a family economy. Over the last century, the world has cut off all three legs. A full 70% of Americans don't expect to inherit anything from their parents.[44] Baby boomers have increased their debt by 59% in the last twelve years, and the average 67-year-old retiree increased debt by 169% over the same time period.[45] The wealthiest generation in this nation's history will have the least inheritance to pass on to their children and grandchildren.

> "A good man leaves an inheritance to his children's children, but the wealth of the sinner is stored up for the righteous." (Prov. 13:22)

The mindset of the retirement generation is nicely encapsulated in the bumper sticker on a great many motorhomes running around the country: "I'm spending my children's inheritance." Life becomes a zero sum game, and reverse mortgages become the rule for the elderly whose generational vision begins to fade (and where men and women live self-oriented lives). Understandably, many families are bound by their circumstances and cannot quite work out a financial inheritance. They may be contributing a great deal to a ministry where they pass an inheritance on to their spiritual children. Nevertheless, there are tremendous opportunities for integrating the generations, caring for our parents and leaving an inheritance for our children and our children's children.

My father lived below the poverty level for most of his life, and still saved a modest inheritance for each of his six children. Most importantly, the spiritual capital passed on to his children by the tremendous sacrifice he made to be home with us during our formative years was the highest value inheritance. Throughout the last 26 years of retirement, dad continued to communicate wisdom to his children and grandchildren on a daily basis through e-mail.

The Context in Which to Disciple as We Walk by the Way

Within the family economy, there are plentiful opportunities for discipleship, family integration, and the preparation of our sons and daughters for their own family economies. Family discipleship and economics conferences held in this country and elsewhere are attracting tens of thousands of interested parents. The benefits of a restored vision of the reintegrated family and the family economy are beginning to emerge:

God's intention for family discipleship is plainly stated in Deuteronomy 6:7-9, but what happens when families do not sit in the house or walk by the way anymore? Modern life has introduced a thousand different means by which the family might be disintegrated. The family is pulled apart by economics, by entertainment, by educational institution (each in his own classroom), by segregated church programs, and so forth. For the first time in 5,900 years, a worldwide social revolution exploded human society and dissolved the family unit. It commenced when fathers left the family farm; then the women joined the work force, and children were shuffled off to age-segregated classrooms and daycare. The effects of such an experiment only become obvious after a few generations. While we do not want to condemn any single part of modern life, the aggregate becomes a problem. The traditions of men begin to displace the law of God (Matt. 15:6), especially in reference to one basic principle found in Deuteronomy 6:7. If family life disintegrates, when would we teach our children God's Word as we sit in the house, as we walk by the way, as rise up, and as we lie down? The first obvious benefit of restoring something of a family economy comes when this father-son, mother-child discipleship actually happens.

There are a myriad of other benefits to realizing and reviving the family economy in the Christian home.

1. Our young daughters need a context in which they may pick up on the Proverbs 31 and Titus 2:4 vision as opposed to the Betty Friedan vision for economy and life. We want to prepare our daughters to hone their God-given abilities to make an economic contribution to their future homes, without losing the vision of a household economy. For some this may very well include a college education, but most colleges have never considered the family economy and a wife's role in it. Before our daughters leave the home, they should learn something of a household economy.

2. Our young men are in desperate need of a household economy, in lieu of learning how to play computer games, develop pornography addictions, and destroy their lives before they get married. If there will be any hope for our young men, their families, and their communities in the future, fathers and faithful men must be more available to disciple and mentor them into life. For the most part, this will be realized through family economies. The situation is utterly desperate, and increasingly families are discovering this to be the only reasonable solution.

Until 1930, almost 75% of young boys (10-15 years of age) were involved in agricultural employment.[46] That number has fallen off to 0.5%, not including the thousands of families that are working on small entrepreneurial ventures in yard maintenance, pet care, and a thousand other little efforts.

3. Instead of turning all of our funding into professional institutions, why not use family economies to care for our elderly parents and grandparents, while providing a practical education and mentorship for our children? As we shall point out in the following chapter, caring for the elderly in our homes could very well save billions of dollars in inheritance for future generations. Moreover, the reintegration of the generations in church and family provides the conveyance of wisdom from elder to younger. This was the major means by which societies were preserved in the past, and this is how another generation will carry on the faith in our day.

4. Over the last thirty years, modern government-enforced insurance programs have increased control over family medical care. Christian families will resist participating in programs that pay for abortion and abortifacient contraceptives. Given the present political environment in this country, the only viable alternative to participating in these programs will be through the Christian medical sharing ministries. Thankfully, these medical sharing programs were exempted in the Affordable Care Act, and many families have saved hundreds of thousands of dollars in insurance premiums over the last twenty years. Companies with less than fifty employees are also exempted, and their employees may avail themselves of these Christian programs.

When socialist governments subsidize medical care they will always ration that care according to their own values and worldview perspective. As socialist medicine is more firmly entrenched, families will have less input in the medical decisions for their own children. When a young Christian couple takes an amniocentesis test and discovers that their child in utero has Downs Syndrome, the future of their child will be more determined by the state than by themselves. The decision concerning medical care for the child is now in the hands of a bureaucrat in a 30-story building in Washington DC, who himself is constrained by 500,000 pages of regulations. The young parents receive the directive: "Abort the child, or the government will provide no funds for its medical care now or later." Unless the family or the church community intervenes in such cases, the child will be aborted. Recent reports from England indicate that 92% of unborn children in England found to have Down Syndrome are aborted.[47]

As Christians encounter schools, corporations, and governments that are increasingly antagonistic to their way of life, they will have to seek out more "islands," more opportunities for family-based business, education, and culture. God has opened up these doors in surprising ways over the last twenty years. Elderly care, online marketing, pet care, contract labor, software development, and a burgeoning service industry all provide decentralized fields of opportunity that were not available to us in the 1990s. Surely, God is protecting His people and He will provide a way for us.

So . . . what have we learned?

1. How does the Proverbs 31 woman look at the money she earns in her family economy?
2. How does the Fourth Commandment speak of the family economy?
3. What is God's creation ordinance for the woman that defines the family economy?
4. Provide several examples of family economies mentioned in

the Bible.

5. How does Betty Friedan's worldview differ from a Christian worldview in regards to the roles of women?
6. What is the English meaning of the Greek word for economics ("oikonomia")?
7. How have families been "individuated" by socialist medicine and economic systems?
8. What are the various elements of a family economy? Give examples of what families can do in work and ministry.
9. What are the three legs on the stool of a family economy?
10. What are the benefits to developing a family economy?

So . . . how are we doing?

1. Have you seen your family disintegrate or re-integrate over the last three years? What does that look like?
2. Describe your family economy. What are ways in which you might create a more robust family economy, where your sons and daughters may be more active in it?

Equip Your Family with These Resources

- **Family Economy**
  www.familyeconomics.com
  Allan Carlson, *The American Way: Family and Community in the Shaping of American Identity* (Intercollegiate Studies Institute, 2003)
- **Mentorship**
  www.ameprogram.com
  Kickstart - Launch Your Life (A Course for Young People) - www.generations.org

6 FAMILY HONOR

Honor your father and your mother: that your days may be long upon the land which the LORD your God gives you. (Ex. 20:12)

It is appropriate to dedicate an entire chapter to this commandment, for our God included this commandment addressed to parents and children in His list of ten.

It is the first commandment with a promise, according to the Apostle Paul, and there are usually temporal benefits that attend this command. When things are not going well for a family, it is plain that they are not enjoying the benefits promised (Eph. 6:2-3). Where there are unhealthy families, disturbed relationships, conflicts, financial crises, divorce, and other family problems, often we do find that a lack of honor is somewhere in the mix. Should a couple come into the church for counsel and fail to follow through on the counsel they are given, one or both of them most likely are dealing with broken relationships with their parents. Very possibly they have failed to honor their parents somewhere along the line. God has hardwired this law into all of human life on this planet. Honor your parents, and things will go well with you on the earth.

What Does This Honor Involve?

The Westminster Larger Catechism Question 127 provides a good summary of the duties required in the Fifth Commandment:

Q. What is the honor that inferiors owe to their superiors?

A. The honor which inferiors owe to their superiors is, all due reverence in heart, word, and behavior; prayer and thanksgiving for them; imitation of their virtues and graces; willing obedience to their lawful commands and counsels; due submission to their corrections; fidelity to, defense, and maintenance of their persons and authority, according to their several ranks, and the nature of their places; bearing with their infirmities, and covering them in love, that so they may be an honor to them and to their government.

There is much to be said about each of these duties, and our time would be well spent in training our children in these. However, the most important thing a parent can do to train his children in honor, is to exemplify honor to their own parents in the presence of their children. I have seen parents who do not reverence their own parents in heart, word, and behavior, deal with unrelenting, difficult rebellion in their own children.

The Hebrew word for honor carries the idea of gravitas or weightiness. Elsewhere, God's law tells us that we should "fear" our father and mother (Lev. 19:3). It is the same word used for fearing and reverencing God (Prov. 1:8, 9:10). Clearly, the application of this honor will vary for a 55-year-old who honors his 85-year-old father as compared to a 2-year-old who honors his 32-year-old mother. There are also differences between cultures, and also between families in regards to how honor is communicated between the generations.

For the purposes of the rest of this chapter, however, we will consider the instruction that our Lord gave in Matthew 15 on honoring parents.

> "Then the scribes and Pharisees who were from Jerusalem came to Jesus, saying, "Why do Your disciples transgress the tradition of the elders? For they do not wash their hands when they eat bread." He answered and said to them, "Why do you also transgress the commandment of God because of your tradition? For God commanded, saying, 'Honor your father and your mother;' and, 'He who curses father or mother, let him be put to death.' But you say, 'Whoever says to his father or mother, "Whatever profit you might have received from me is a gift to God"—then he need not honor his father or mother.' Thus you have made the commandment of God of no effect by your tradition." (Matt. 15:1-6)

There can be no question that Jesus Christ had immense respect for this commandment from God. Some mistakenly believe that Jesus took issue with the Pharisees for their over-emphasis on God's laws. But actually, His issue with them was the opposite. He was concerned about their failure to respect the law of God, their avoidance of the core issues, and their lifting up of human traditions in primacy over the commands of God. In this case, the Jewish leaders had institutionalized an approach to tithing (and giving to the temple) that exempted their followers from providing for the needs of their parents in their old age. They called this "social security" program "Corban." In so doing they had disregarded the law of God and encouraged others to break this holy commandment.

The Example of Christ

So great was Jesus' love for this commandment that He exemplified obedience to it on the cross. When we consider the importance of the Person of Christ as the very, eternal Son of God; and as we think of the importance of the cross where He redeemed His people and died for the sins of the world; we can only stand in wonder at these words in John 19. As He hung there in agony, Christ looked down upon His mother and said,

"Woman, behold your son!"

Then He looked down upon His disciple, John, and said,

"Behold, your mother!"

Does this digression seem a little incongruous, superfluous, or even unintentional? A non sequitur? How does this fit into the scene that represents the greatest event in all of human history? Why does the Redeemer of the world stop the action for a moment to provide for the care of His aging mother by transferring responsibility to John?

If we are to have the same mind of Christ (Phil. 2:4), and "walk just as he walked" (1 John 2:6), then this short digression has immense meaning to every person who ever had a mother or a father in the world. There on the cross, our Lord honored His mother. He understood the will of the Father (Ps. 40:8, John 4:34), and the will of the Father is to take responsibility for the care of one's aging parents (Matt. 15:1-6).

We also learn that the priorities of Jesus are not always our priorities or those priorities imposed on us by the world. In another passage that informs us concerning that momentous, final day in which the Son of Man will judge the world (Matt. 25:31-46), Christ gives us more insight into the matters of the utmost importance. He does not mention the finer points of doctrine, eschatology, ecclesiology, or even soteriology. Nothing is said about who we voted for or how much we complained about politics. Nor is there any mention of how many people were evangelized under our ministry work. What seems to be of the greatest concern in the day of judgment is whether we have reached out to the "least of Christ's brothers." Did we feed the hungry, clothe the naked, and visit the sick and those in prison? What is of essence to Christ is our relationship with Him and with His friends.

The Pharisees had developed a human tradition (or shall we call it an "institution?") whereby they could exempt a person from the obligation to care for his or her aging parents. Somehow, taking personal care of one's own parents had dropped off the priority list of the Pharisees. They lost sight of the will of God for family life. How does this same thing happen to us in the flurry of all of our systems, traditions, programs, institutions, and bureaucracies? Has the modern social security system relieved us somewhat of our personal responsibility to our parents in their old age?

There should be no question that God feels strongly about this matter of caring for elderly parents. In what might be the most emphatic language used in the entire New Testament, the Apostle Paul refers to the man who is unwilling to care for his widowed mother or grandmother as "worse than an unbeliever" (1 Tim. 5:8). It seems the Apostle considers such flagrant irresponsibility worthy of church discipline (also reference 2 Thess. 3:10-15). Christian family eldercare is Christianity 101.

Modern humanist philosophers love their institutional form of love, funded by government dollars. Like the archetypal humanist and socialist, Jean-Jacques Rousseau they consider themselves the greatest lovers who ever lived, but they fail at love. Rousseau abandoned his five children upon their births, at the steps of an orphanage where they almost certainly died, because he did not wish to care for his own children. He was too busy "saving the world." Karl Marx starved his own children to death,[48] and then introduced a socialist system that was supposed to be the incarnation of love on earth.

The Traditions of Men

The year 2011 was something of a symbolic year in the history of the United States. It was the year that the Social Security Fund went into the red, where it has remained ever since. The Social Security System was developed as a sophisticated Ponzi scheme, always relying on a positive birth replacement rate and a strong worker-to-retiree ratio. The timing for the bust of Social Security could not have been worse, because 2011 was also the year that the first Baby Boomers entered their retirement years. Between 2011 and 2029, eighty million Baby Boomers will have retired, and over the next thirty-five years they will require a high level of economic support before they die. Since 1960, this Baby Boom generation also instigated an abortion holocaust that has resulted in 80 million dead babies in this country alone. Now, who will support these retirees through the 2050s? In this country, expect the worker-to-retiree ratio in 2030 to be one-third of what it was in 1950 when social security was first implemented.[49]

Even more important for our consideration, what is the condition of the character of the younger generation? Will the few young people left be able to support the heavy load of elderly retirees and a bankrupt Social Security system? Will they live self-sacrificially and double their efforts to make up for the slack in the retirement funds? Regrettably, the timing for this system failure could not be worse. *Time Magazine* recently reported the Millennial generation to be the laziest, the unluckiest, and the most narcissistic generation ever.[50] As we know, over half of children born to women under thirty years of age are born out of wedlock.[51] If the majority of young men refuse to act the father for their own children in 2016, why would they care for the elderly in 2036? The masses of young men are playing their computer games while empires burn to the ground around them (a pattern seen in the fall of Rome in the 4th and 5th centuries). But what lesson did the Baby Boomers pass along when they aborted eighty million siblings of those who will operate the economy in the year 2030? These young people, on average, start out with less capital than any previous generation, and they are saddled with three hundred times more college debt than the Gen X'ers in the 1970s and 1980s.[52] Meanwhile, the Baby Boomers retire with far more debt than the Silent generation and very little, if any, inheritance to pass along.[53] This is what you get when a nation seeps in self-centered narcissism, materialism, and socialism over half a century. This experiment with socialism will not bode well for the future. What will the most narcissistic generation do to the 80 million Baby Boomers that contributed to 80 million abortions between 1970 and 2000? Mass euthanasia appears to be the only probable political "solution," given the present economy, social conditions, and moral perspectives of the developing generation.

Highly institutionalized and socialized elder care is already proving itself unwieldy. Over the next 25 years, the 75-years-old-and-older population will grow from 20 million to 46 million.[54] Already, half of unmarried retirees rely upon social security almost exclusively. The Congressional Budget Office is proposing a 29% cut in the average social security check by the year 2029.[55] If the average elder care facility runs $3,000 per month, the $900 Social Security check will hardly cover a fraction of the cost.

The degree to which euthanasia is employed will depend on whether the state rations the medicine. However, here is the conundrum. As the patients progress in years they require more care, but they have less money to pay for it. Other "more viable" patients will be considered more qualified for the rationed care, and the others will be left to die. As socialist systems run out of "other people's money," it will revert to providing the least common denominator care for the masses—and euthanasia will soon follow.

In so many ways, professionals, bureaucrats, government-funded programs, and quid-pro-quo business arrangements have displaced opportunities for personal service and expressions of love. Billions of dollars of inheritance that would have been passed on to children have been transferred to the state.

The next twenty years will be the most defining years in this nation's history, as we will witness massive socio-economic changes. The important question for us, however, is this: Will family relationships disintegrate across the generations, or will families re-integrate the generations? Will the relationships between children, parents, and grandparents become closer or farther apart? Will we find cross-generational churches, where the 80-year-old and the 8-year-old sit in the same pew? Now is the time to restore relationships across the generations. There is no better way to do this than by restoring home-based eldercare as the Lord leads in various families across this country and around the world.

While the socialist governments always run out of resources, the love of Christ will not. Nothing can compete with voluntary, sacrificial, compassionate, relational love. We have no fear that this love will bear all things, believe all things, hope all things, and endure all things. It is a thousand times more robust than the federal government's Department of Health and Human Services. The powerful motive of love trumps the motive of capitalistic greed and the motive behind the power-driven, big government state. The cold dystopian world of socialism and Jean-Jacques Rousseau must go. It is wilting away, and it will die.

The biblical approach to helping the poor never endorses the Marxist model of forced redistribution of wealth. Biblical charity is local, voluntary, and relational (Deut. 14:28-29). Jesus commended the good Samaritan who reached for his own wallet to help the stranded and wounded traveler (Luke 10:25-37). James commended the personal visitation of the poor in James 1:27. And the Apostle Paul required the family to be the first to care for the widowed mother and grandmother, and for her to only resort to the church if the family was unable to provide the care. He makes no mention of the state.

How to Honor Your Parents in Their Later Years

At this crucial time in history, Christian families are restoring the biblical vision for family eldercare. They are bringing their own aging parents into their homes. Many churches minister to nursing homes on a weekly basis. This is what will mark out true Christian faith in future years. As Christians are really starting to care for the "least of these, my brethren" (Matt. 25:40b), the stories of sacrificial love for aging parents abound. Christian families understand the limitations of bureaucracies and institutionalized care that rests on a quid-pro-quo business model. They begin to see the blessings of living in relationship with the older generations.

Here are a few examples of how Christian families can show honor to their aging parents:

1. Call them, write to them, and visit them on a regular basis.
2. Invite them to live with you, even if you know they will refuse it.
3. Move your family in order to be closer to them, so you can be more available to help them.
4. Adapt your home with architectural improvements and ergonomic conveniences to make them more comfortable.
5. Pray for them.
6. Help them to their medical appointments.
7. Encourage your children to spend time with them.
8. Glean from their wisdom and capitalize on their gifts.
9. Send money for their upkeep if they run short on funds.
10. Help them with difficult tasks, home repairs, and so forth.

While it can be a challenge to provide for unbelieving parents or grandparents, we are still obligated to show them honor. I recommend that those living in a Christian home participate at some level in daily family devotions and weekly church worship (as the members of the home are physically able.) Where unbelieving relatives cannot comply with this, some accommodation may have to be made in living arrangements. Perhaps the physical separation of living quarters may be in order. Unbelieving grandparents actually do have some wisdom to share with their grandchildren, but Christian parents should be careful to provide necessary oversight as those primarily responsible for their children's nurture.

In many cases, aging parents are not willing to live with their adult children even when invited. This is more common in societies where government-installed institutions have reigned supreme for several generations and relationships have become cold and distant. People enjoy living alone. Seven times the percentage of people live alone today than at the turn of the 20th century.[57] Governments supply social security support, parents burn up their kids' inheritance, children are raised in government-funded programs, marriages break up in divorce, and relationships dry up over the years. Often, unresolved conflicts, bitterness, and pride create great rifts in relationships. Under such conditions, we cannot expect much to change outside of the supernatural work of God changing hearts and restoring relationships. Continue to pray over these things, and wait in hope for God's great work!

Benefits of Christian Family Eldercare

There are many wonderful benefits of home-based elder care, most of which are on the intangible side. The world doesn't understand these intangibles. How can a thousand hours of back-breaking, sacrificial service result in blessings? We must have a God who can supernaturally turn sacrifice into blessing.

On the tangible side, think of the billions and trillions of dollars that could be saved for inheritance if we could just restore relationships between the generations. The Apostle Paul considered this to be normal part of family life:

> "For the children ought not to lay up for the parents, but the parents for the children." (2 Cor. 12:14b)

Assisted living centers currently cost an average of $36,000 per person per year and ($50,000 for the patient with Dementia). Social security remuneration averages $16,000 per year (at $1,335 per month). Assuming there are eighty million retirees from the Baby Boom generation by the 2020s, that's $2.9 trillion in inheritance turned over to basic institutional care every year. If families provided much of that care instead, then as much as $60 trillion of potential inheritance could flow back into these individual family units (which would enable families to provide a better start for their Millennials).

This reintegration of the generations into the home will also provide ample opportunity for the transfer of wisdom. When the elderly generation takes the time to share their wisdom and the younger generation is humble and receives it, the results are nothing short of phenomenal. This may be the only saving grace left for the present social milieu. If by God's grace, millions of families across the nation and within the Christian community would reintegrate the generations, an entire civilization would be salvaged. This is the secret weapon contained in the fifth commandment. It is the means by which society is able to continue on the earth. Without the hearts of fathers and grandfathers turning towards their sons and grandsons, and the hearts of sons and grandsons turning towards their fathers and grandfathers, we will have to expect God to revisit the world with a curse (Mal. 4:6). These foreboding words make up the final revelation contained in the Old Testament. May God have mercy on our families and our communities in this generation.

Conclusion

Obviously, every family will encounter their own unique circumstances, but in any case the purpose of this chapter is to encourage more honor and more building of good relationships across the generations. I urge the reader to regain something of the vision that was lost over previous generations, by exploring resources and conferences on this subject. Visit elderly care facilities in the area of your home on a weekly or monthly basis, and establish long-term relationships with the residents. Use Skype or other means to re-connect on a regular basis with grandparents who don't live nearby. Be sure that your aging parents know that your home is available to them should they need more regular care. Seek God's will in these things, and follow the example of our Savior on the cross when He made special provision for His own mother with the disciple whom He loved.

So . . . what have we learned?

1. How did Jesus keep the fifth commandment while He was on the cross?
2. What was the Pharisees' system of Corban?
3. What are some of the ways that children should honor their parents, as described in the Westminster Larger Catechism?
4. How does the Apostle Paul interpret this principle of honor in 1 Timothy 5?
5. What does the Word of God say about the care of widows and orphans? To whom do these responsibilities belong? How does this contrast with the socialist approach?
6. What are the tangible and intangible benefits of family-based eldercare?
7. What are the various economic and social stresses upon the current social security system?

8. What is the promise contained in the fifth commandment? What is the curse contained in Malachi 4:6?

So . . . how are we doing?

1. What are your plans for caring for your aging parents? What are the conditions under which you might take them into your home? Would they agree to this? In what ways would home care be an improvement over institutional care? What are the benefits of institutional, professional care?
2. What are your plans towards saving an inheritance for your children? Have you conveyed your plans concerning your own care to your children?

Equip Your Family with These Resources

-   www.ChristianFamilyEldercare.org
    Marcia Washburn, *Home-based Eldercare: Stories and Strategies for Caregivers*
-   Peter Rosenberger, *Wear Comfortable Shoes: Surviving and Thriving as a Caregiver*

7 FAMILY CULTURE

The breakdown of the family has necessarily led to a breakdown of culture. For centuries, God preserved the various cultures of the nations around the world by His common grace through the institution of the family. At first, socialist governments, industrialized economies, and centralized control of education, media, and the arts displaced family and family culture. Given that marriage and family is God's means of preserving human society in His common grace, the weakening of the family will eventually produce the breakdown of human civilization. As the family breaks down, so do the arts, the customs, and the social institutions of the nations. There is symbiosis between family and culture, because the family is meant to be the basic social unit and cultural institution of every society. This modern experiment that so uprooted the family will not end well.

As Christian families however, we have a vested interest in salvaging marriage, family, and culture for our grandchildren and great grandchildren. We have a vision and a kingdom to pass on to the next generation. We seek and expect the blessing of God upon our children unto thousands of generations, as we love Him and keep His commandments (Ex. 20:6). We hope that our children will be "mighty in the earth" (Ps. 112:1-2) as we fear God and delight greatly in His commandments.

Culture is defined as "the customs, arts, social institutions, and achievements of a particular nation, people, or other social group."[58] Human culture is not neutral. Some cultures, art forms, and customs are better than others in that they better reflect obedience to the commandments of God. When cultures and customs counter God's Word in the most egregious ways, they become destructive to their respective social groups.

The Cultural Commandment

Indeed, God has something to say about human culture. Given the temporal blessing attached to it, the Fifth Commandment retains an important cultural connotation. I like to call it "the cultural commandment. This command already discussed in Chapter 6 has tremendous, all-encompassing import upon cultures. Where the commandment is obeyed, healthy sustainable culture develops. Where the commandment is disobeyed, things will not go well in the culture that develops (Deut. 5:16). How does a culture degrade from Isaac Watts and Bach who were the favorite composers in the 1740s to Eminem and Katy Perry who are the favorite composers and artists of our day? It should be fairly obvious that there is something of a retrograde from "Jesu, Joy of Man's Desiring" and "Oh, for a Thousand Tongues to Sing" to Eminem's compositions that refer to his own mother as a female dog. The decline is religious, moral, and cultural. The breakdown of culture happens with the aggregate loss of honor for parents, generation by generation. Conversely, healthy sustainable cultures are developed when men and women begin to obey the Fifth Commandment again. This can only happen where families exist and where there are parents to honor.

> My son, keep your father's command, and do not forsake the law of your mother. Bind them continually upon your heart; tie them around your neck. When you roam, they will lead you; when you sleep, they will keep you; and when you awake, they will speak with you. (Prov. 6:20-22)

The Proverbs speak of honoring a mother's commandments, and we understand that there is some distinction between God's commandments and a mother's commandments. Mothers tell children to tuck in their shirts, make their beds, do their chores, to not run out into a busy street, and to turn down the music. This constitutes the wisdom of a mother and her best applications of God's commandments. Whether she is a believer or not, she wants the best for her child. A good mother doesn't want her child to live a life of dishonor, dishonesty, and slothfulness, so she will teach her children these character traits using the best applications she can think of. As her child grows up and leaves the house, he ought to continue honoring his mother's wisdom. Perhaps he may find better ways to incorporate God's commandments into his life and culture, but his mother gives him a good place to start.

There are aspects of culture that are relativistic, I grant, but much of culture can be governed by the absolutes that come by way of God's laws. Christians today like to point out that there is very little in the Bible regulating music, dress, manners, art, and other forms of culture. They would condemn parents who teach their children to tuck in their shirts, say "Yes Sir; no Sir," and turn down the music. They frown on parents who attempt to share wisdom relating to dress or music with their teen children. These professing Christians ignore the Fifth Commandment and the importance of parents in forming, preserving, and developing human culture.

When young people ask me whether they should listen to this or that style of music, I respond with a simple question. "What do your parents think about this music or that music?" If they say that their parents like this artist but not that one, this album but not that one, and this album cut but not that one, I tell them to go with their parents' advice. "Honor your father and mother." It is a very simple answer, a principled answer, and a well-grounded answer to every question relating to culture. Children whose parents are not believers will have to seek wisdom from their spiritual fathers and mothers, elders in the church and disciplers who can give them guidance in cultural matters. Nevertheless, even non-Christian parents have a compendium of wisdom that should be heeded by their children in any case. Few parents in the world are void of absolutely any wisdom at all. Age provides more wisdom, and we find ourselves standing on our parents' shoulders as the years go by. We honor whatever wisdom God has given our parents in theology, manners, music, hygiene, and household habits. Hopefully, we will grow from that reservoir of wisdom and improve on it in our later years.

I am careful not to condemn any certain form of music. However, I believe that some forms would quickly disappear if a culture of honor existed between the generations. Wholesome, constructive, and sustainable forms of artistic expression tend to survive through the generations.

Of course, all of God's commandments are key to developing healthy culture in the home and society. The most important foundational element for all of Christian culture in the home is the First Commandment. It is always beneficial to ask the question: does this cultural experience contribute in any way to the fear of God in my life and in my family?

The Challenges Every Family Faces

Families, whether Christian or not, have always faced the problem of sin: hatred, bitterness, strife, infidelity, abuse, anger, and envy. Sin is nothing new. The modern family, however, faces increased external pressures that are brought by extremely powerful cultural systems and the general weakness of the entire structure of the family unit (a phenomena that has emerged over the last five generations). These systems have accelerated apostasy and prevented faith continuity and family solidarity through the generations. It becomes abundantly obvious to recent immigrants who started with intact families and faith, and moved their families into developed nations. Within a single generation, they wake up to discover family integrity and faith severely eroded.

Modern life introduces more challenges to family culture by offering to teens especially far more time for leisure. Add to this a huge increase in disposable income and the younger generation comes to expect constant access to entertainment. This is the major impediment to maturation and marriage for our young adults.

Until the compulsory attendance laws were completely instituted and large government schools put in place (by the 1930s), children were educated in homes and one-room school houses. Children worked side by side with their parents in the fields. As late as the 1940s, young boys like Johnny Cash worked long hours with their parents trying to sustain a barely viable family economy. Singer/Songwriter Cash had no regrets as he testifies in his autobiography before he died,

> Inside me, my boyhood feels so close, but when I look around, it seems to belong to a vanished world. In the United States in the late 1990s, is it really possible to imagine families, boys and girls of eight to eighteen at their parents' sides in the cotton fields, working through the July heat from dawn

to dusk, driving away exhaustion with songs of the spirit? Are there still places where a young boy can leave his house after breakfast with just a fishing pole and spend the whole day rambling and adventuring alone, unsupervised and un-afraid, trusted and un-feared for? Perhaps there are. I hope so. But I suspect otherwise. I think that even if such places do exist, our televisions have blinded us to them.[59]

In fifty years, everything has changed. Family economies are now hardly a consideration in the minds of most fathers and mothers (let alone in practice).

Since the 1940s, the culture of the teenager has been developed by the peer group and pop culture influence. For 5,940 years of world history, children adopted the music, the clothing, and the manners of their parents. When Laura Ingalls Wilder's "Pa" would play "Yan-kee Doodle" and "Old Dan Tucker" on the fiddle during the long winter nights by the fireplace in the 1890s, the children would dance around the living room. This was how folk culture progressed from one generation to the next, until 1940. With the new media of the AM and FM radio, and the large age-segregated classrooms, an entire-ly new approach to human culture began on planet earth. Powerful principalities worked through highly centralized media sources in Hollywood and Nashville to produce media staples for the masses. Junior high and high school children attended large schools and spent long hours with their peer groups, and almost every mem-ber of the peer group had access to the radio, and eventually other forms of media as well. From these influences, 90-99% of the pop-ulace formed their culture, their music, their dress, their lifestyle, their social system, and their politics. It was "pop" culture—gener-ally transient, disposable, isolating, degrading, de-humanizing, and deconstructive.

During this time, pastors had very little influence on the culture of their congregants. If a youth pastor stepped out in front of his congregation and noted that they all had bones in their noses, he would immediately shove a bone through his nose (to be relevant). The culture and the worldview of the society around his congregation had already been formed by popular culture, and the pastor feels compelled to conform to it.

Leading the culture at the top of the pyramid of the movers and shakers, one does not find the wisdom of Jonathan Edwards, John Owen, George Washington, George Whitefield, Martin Luther, or even John Milton or William Shakespeare. Instead, we find the sage examples of Lady Gaga, Eminem, Miley Cyrus, Psy, and Robert Downey, Jr. These, and those who write their scripts, are the leaders.

> "He who walks with wise men will be wise, but the companion of fools will be destroyed." (Prov. 13:20)

The Further Challenges Modern Society Faces

Much of modern culture has devolved into sheer entertainment and escapism. Man has become "lost in the metaphor." No longer does the metaphor lead him to truth, to a real grasp on reality, and to the betterment of his knowledge and life. Popluar culture has taken on a single use—escape.

The mode of culture and media itself becomes a means of isolation. Jean-Paul Sartre, the famous existentialist, dreamed of a world where man could isolate himself from the "hell of other people," hermetically sealed off forever. This we have virtually accomplished with our individual iPhones, iPods, iPads, and other iGadgets. I remember the first time somebody gave me an iPod. My wife and I went away on an overnight date, and there I was listening to music through the headphones, in my own world. It was not satisfying for me, so I purchased a dual earphone jack and we could both listen at the same time. I had turned the all-about-mePod into a wePod!

Modern culture seems to center around personal electronic devices now. Each person is expected to create his/her online pseudo-personality using social media. Young people are seen in restaurants texting each other. It has the appearance of a cold, dead, sterile world, void of relationship. The isolation is chronic, acute, agonizing, unbearable to anybody who lives a little west of Eden. Cain wanders as a vagabond east of Eden, alone in the wasteland of post-modern death.

Of all of the modern forms of isolation, the most obviously devastating medium is online pornography. It is depersonalized sexuality gone mainstream. As I mentioned earlier, at least eighty percent of young men 18-25 years of age are addicted to pornography, accessing it on a weekly or monthly basis.[60] One porn site claims 259 million subscribers, and online porn use has quadrupled in four years.[61] While some percentage of these addicts will certainly find deliverance by the Gospel of Jesus Christ, the consequences of this scourge are yet to be seen. What will this electronic experiment in isolation and perversion produce? The damage upon future marital relationships, the lowering of the marriage rate itself, and the additional sexual perversions and sexual nihilism still to come is all too much to fathom. The concern for the Christian community is real and urgent, especially for our young men. Without a radical shift in the way we disciple our young men, handle electronic media, and organize our social situations, we can expect that Christian families will follow the trends of the world. In the words of Jesus Christ, unless we repent, we shall likewise perish (Luke 13:3,5). These words take on new meaning for a deconstructing Western world.

Where there is no active family economy and where the entertainment culture predominates, expect nothing but retrograde in the character of the youth and the nation. Young people who are saturated in games, pornography, texting, music, and movies will have lost all sense of what it is to be productive in an economy. Slothfulness will be the rule of the day, and future families will languish for lack of responsible fathers and mothers.

The Challenges Facing the Christian Community

If, by the grace of God, we have avoided some of the larger problems facing the modern culture, there are still a number of challenges that face our Christian families and communities.

Most churches have found that they simply cannot survive unless they adopt the cultural idiom in their music. While pastors and elders (rightly) hesitate to bind the consciences of their people to only listen to certain forms of music, they still must choose a form around which the entire congregation can unite and participate when they gather to worship. A few churches resort to the old hymns and traditional forms, but these congregations usually lose the younger crowd since they are acclimating themselves to the latest pop form played on the local FM radio stations.

Revolutionary culture is making dramatic changes in our church communities every ten or twenty years now. Hardly any churches sing the Vineyard songs from the 1980s or the Maranatha songs from the 1970s anymore. Whereas culture used to develop gradually, and powerful, inspirational hymns written 200-1000 years earlier would strengthen the Church and be passed on from generation to generation, that has not been happening since 1970. Churches now hold traditional services for the elders and contemporary services for the twenty-somethings. No longer do the older women teach the younger women, and the older men guide the younger men according to the Titus 2 model. Great grandparents almost never worship in the same church with their great grandchildren. Every generation feels they must develop their own church and culture in the revolution. The strength that comes by generational connection and by a culture of honor dissipates, and the Church slowly breaks down.

The music played during celebratory events like weddings is usually a hodgepodge of various forms, or a form to which the rest of the community cannot relate. Thus, the popular revolutionary culture leaves the Church in a cultural disunity. The revolution has not subsided any for fifty years.

Families that choose to develop their own culture will typically find themselves in isolation to some degree. They struggle to find any cultural unity with other families. Unless they can find unity in Jesus Christ, they find themselves living at a distance from other families in the community. Of course, they can still serve others, especially those in need, and they can exercise love for their brothers and sisters in tangible ways. If families protest the dominant cultural idioms (especially in music), they will have a hard time forming any other unity in form with the rest of the church community.

We do want to allow Christian liberty for other families when they have different standards for their music, movies, etc. To enforce our standards on other families would be a violation of jurisdiction. While we do our best to make wise decisions for our own family, we must be careful to provide liberty to others. It is easy to become judgmental or proud. Every family develops different habits, different fences, different disciplines, and different schedules. They may make good decisions in some areas and bad decisions in others. While you may feel that you have carefully dialed in some area better than the next family, be careful. We must avoid comparing our families in aggregate with others and thinking that we have excelled the others. We are all subject to the same biblical principles, and it is always better to find unity in these principles. In your conversations, spend less time discussing your own particular applications, and always return to the root biblical principles that govern all of us.

Music has come to dominate in church and religion over the last generation or two. Where the preaching once guided the congregation and remained central in the service, now the "praise and worship" music program took its place. Romanticism insisted that feelings and experience dominate the religious experience. Emotion liberated man from the "domination of reason." While not every expression of the modern church has capitulated to romanticism and the dominance of emotion, the winds of the zeitgeist blow hard. Scripture insists that the understanding and the inner being of the spirit be both engaged in the music.

> "What is the conclusion then? I will pray with the spirit, and I will also pray with the understanding. I will sing with the spirit, and I will also sing with the understanding." (1 Cor. 14:15)

Also, Colossians 3:16 presents the purpose of our music in the community of believers as admonishment and teaching. Music ought to be primarily an intellectual experience during which we are receiving teaching and admonishment concerning certain truths, doctrines, and commands from the Word of God. That may sound strange to the modern ear, but that's because we have grown up in a period when the worldview of romanticism rules. The Greek god Dionysus, known as the god of excess and emotion, dominates in almost every avenue of culture today, including the Church.

Families should also be acutely aware of the worldviews that dominate the mass culture today. The resources at the end of this chapter should help in that regard. Unless families are carefully trained to recognize existentialism, nihilism, pluralism, materialism, romanticism, or relativism, they should stay away from almost all of the popular movies and music in this culture. We must be prepared to cast down "arguments and every high thing that exalts itself against the knowledge of God, bringing every thought into captivity to the obedience of Christ" (2 Cor. 10:5). Of course, these arguments and imaginations are everywhere around us, especially in popular culture. If popular culture bears more influence than pastors, then worldly thinking will naturally infect entire church congregations within a decade or so. But where pastors and parents are engaging the battle and critiquing the culture on a constant basis, there will be hope that the faith will be preserved.

Biblical Principles in Relation to Music, Manners, Dress, Celebrations, and Entertainment

> "One person esteems one day above another; another esteems every day alike. Let each be fully convinced in his own mind. He who observes the day, observes it to the Lord; and he who does not observe the day, to the Lord he does not observe it. He who eats, eats to the Lord, for he gives God thanks; and he who does not eat, to the Lord he does not eat, and gives God thanks. For none of us lives to himself, and no one dies to himself. For if we live, we live to the Lord; and if we die, we die to the Lord. Therefore, whether we live or die, we are the Lord's." (Rom. 14:5-8)

According to this passage, the grand principle governing family celebrations and culture is thanksgiving. It is living to love the Lord, to praise the Lord, to talk of the Lord, and to thank the Lord. If our entertainment and celebrations do not yield this, we are not creating a Christian culture in our homes.

Several years ago, I began to notice that we had taken on a dualism in family life. We would worship God on Sundays, during family devotions, and before the meals. Yet, it seemed we were reticent to thank God for snacks, for movies, for entertainment, and for marital intimacy as a couple. Why is it this way in so many homes? Entertainment has itself become a form of idolatry in modern life, and Christians are too quick to participate in it. Thankfully, we do come to see the futility and damaging fruits of this idolatry. We simply cannot tolerate these idols competing with our worship of the true of living God in our homes. Any pleasurable experience loses its luster when we have no gratitude for the Giver. Our best moments cease to be our best moments, if we are not praising Jesus.

The Old Testament also offers two related principles to frame our vacations and entertainment, in Deuteronomy 16:

> "You shall rejoice before the Lord your God, you and your son and your daughter, your male servant and your female servant, the Levite who is within your gates, the stranger and the fatherless and the widow who are among you, at the place where the Lord your God chooses to make His name abide." (Deut. 16:11)

In the Old Testament economy, rejoicing and celebration was not optional. God commanded His people to rejoice and to celebrate, but they were to do it 1) in community and 2) before the Lord. Old Testament Israelite families would spend 10% of their annual income on the "rejoicing" tithe, set aside to feast in community in the presence of the Lord. These principles must be applied to family feasts, family games, family music, and family celebrations of all kinds. What a contrast with the isolation, the self-centeredness, the ingratitude, and the misery of the modern entertainment culture! It truly is miserable. One need only study the faces of the entertainment-saturated youth hanging out the shopping malls today to see the misery of it all.

Nevertheless, the problem of the modern world remains the problem of excess. As Neil Postman put it a generation ago, we are "entertaining ourselves to death." For several years, my family has had a sign posted on the refrigerator containing sage wisdom from Leonard Ravenhill: "Entertainment is the devil's substitute for joy." It is a good reminder. While vacation and celebration make up an occasional part of the Christian life (something like three weeks out of every year), the assumption is that we are working six days a week. Work and worship are the warp and the woof of the Christian home.

Build Your Family Culture

I cannot think of another solution for salvaging culture and restoring biblical living to the modern age than to return to a family-driven culture. As millions of families deliberately purpose to create culture in their homes based upon God's Word, a sustainable culture and a continuity of generational faith will emerge. This can happen even in the modern day.

Several years ago, I asked my father why he decided to take his family to the mission field in Japan in 1969. His answer surprised me. As he worked as a public school teacher and a Christian school teacher through the 1950s and 1960s, he watched teen culture develop, he saw the cultural revolution mature, he witnessed the rise of secular materialism, and he saw evolution dominate in the public schools. By 1969, he came to the conclusion that he did not want to raise us in this new secular culture. He wanted to preach the Gospel to the Japanese, but he also wanted to get his children out of American culture to create his own family culture, and this he did. We were homeschooled in that little house in Karatsu on the southern island, Kyushu. We read together in the living room during the long winter nights. We worshiped God together as a family every morning. We passed out tens of thousands of tracts to the Japanese during the festivals. We had zero access to Western media, except for occasional newscasts from American military radio stations. We played baseball and football in the rice paddies, and hiked the mountains surrounding the villages where we lived. My father taught us Greek, home repair, and theology in the living room. He involved us in the family business of publishing. He bought an organ kit and I remember soldering the capacitors and the resistors on the boards to produce a fine instrument mom would play on Sundays for worship. My father worked hard on this creative vision for the family and he sacrificed much to create a unique family culture for us. To this day, I believe this has contributed greatly to sustaining the faith and strengthening the solidarity of the family through the generations (at least in one family's experience).

Here are several practical suggestions for modern families as they set out to build their own culture in the 21st Century:

1. Unplug the earbuds. If you're listening to recorded music, let the whole family enjoy it. You will be amazed how this will transform the music tastes in your home, if it becomes the default habit for listening to music over a period of several years. When a Christian family listens to music in community (or in relationship with loved ones), new standards and habits will naturally develop over time.

What is your ratio of individualized entertainment to cultural experiences in community? Do your children spend twenty hours a week with their iPods, iPads, and iPhones, and only one hour a week gathered in the living room singing together in community? Read out loud, sing out loud, and rejoice in community, coram Deo (in the presence of God).

I make it a point to watch movies with my children and we all carefully critique it afterwards. We acknowledge the positive points in which common grace has sanctified culture, thanks to the influence of 2,000 years of Christ and the Gospel. Then, we interact with the problems in the film in the area of worldview, ethics, attitudes, outcomes, and mode.

2. Be aware of what media is doing to you and to your family. Of course, parental example is most important. For the last five years, I have avoided earphones and earbuds as much as possible and this has contributed something to my cultural preferences.

Several years ago, we took a media fast for several months staying away from all electronic media, music, movies, and games. These fasts help us to see what the media has done to us or what it is doing to us. We begin to see where sensuality, idolatry, addictions, and isolation have infected us.

Our children are watching us and they will discern our chief loves. If we prefer worship and the fellowship of believers over isolation and entertainment, they will know it. If we are constantly absorbed in the electronic universe, performing endless web searches, and operating internet games and applications, they will get the message.

3. Make good choices for entertainment and cultural experiences based on these three tests.

Check your motive. Am I participating in this activity as an expression of love for God, and in appreciation for His good gifts? Or, am I far less likely to offer prayers of thanksgiving now that I am in this movie theater? Will this quench my love for God? Am I doing this out of gratitude, love for God, and fear of God?

Check the content of the entertainment itself. Does this conform to a biblical world and life view at all levels or at any level? Or does this musical piece or motion picture encourage the breaking of God's laws with impunity?

> "Finally, brethren, whatever things are true, whatever things are noble, whatever things are just, whatever things are pure, whatever things are lovely, whatever things are of good report, if there is any virtue and if there is anything praiseworthy—meditate on these things." (Phil. 4:8)

Check the effect of the cultural experience. Do the particular entertainment forms and the extent to which your family participates yield good effects on you and your family? Does watching a marathon of five James Bond movies on a Saturday prepare you well for the worship of God on the Lord's Day? Do you find that a constant regimen of the Disney channel all day long produces the fruits of the Spirit in your children? Does this entertainment edify your family?

"Let all things be done unto edification." (1 Cor. 14:26b)

4. Be particularly careful to avoid immersing your family in excessive amounts of entertainment. If we are spending more time in secular entertainment (where man, not God, is glorified), our family members will begin to lose a taste for the worship of God. What is the ratio of "pure entertainment" to worship, in your family? Is it 20 hours of entertainment to 1 hour of worship, or the other way around? Should you discover that your children have little taste for worship, most likely it is because they are completely saturated in entertainment.

5. Also, double check the ratio of time your family spends working, against the time spent with entertainment. Again, work-to-play ratios should come out to 5 to 1 or even 10 to 1 versus the other way around. Families may have to revive more family economy and service if they find they have an excessive play-to-work ratio.

6. Of all of the modes of cultural experience, modern music and film are the most emotive. Certainly, we want our emotions engaged in our cultural experiences, but only in the right proportion and the right direction. Do the entertainment choices in your home play on emotions more than they engage the mind? When we sing in church are we more into the emotive effect, or are we struck by the meaning of the words of the psalms, hymns, and spiritual songs that we sing? "I will sing with the spirit, and I will also sing with the understanding" (1 Cor. 14:15b). Both the intellect and the emotions (and the all encompassing spirit in the innermost being) should be equally engaged in this worship.

7. Watch for escapism. Excessive use of fiction literature, especially the science fiction and fantasy genres, can form those exit ramps off the highway of reality. Are we using entertainment to escape reality,

(God being the ultimate essence of that reality and the very source)?

8. Control access to the media when your children are young, and teach responsible use of the media tools. Delaying access to hand-held web devices is often a very good idea. Normally, you don't give a two-year-old a chain saw for his birthday, and you don't put an eight year old behind the wheel of a car. A due respect for the potential dangers with the internet would urge the utmost caution with its use. At the minimum, every device in the home should be monitored by Covenant Eyes or some similar application. We are however, most concerned that our teenaged children love God with all their hearts, all their minds, and all their strength. We want them to exercise the fruit of the spirit of self-control, and make wise choices for themselves. As my children approach 16-18 years of age, I have moderated control over their cultural choices. Only so much micromanaging is effective if their hearts are not changed.

Should young teens in the home begin to make characteristically bad choices, or should they exhibit patterns of deception, some correction is most certainly in order. Given that communication pathways are still available with these young teens, parents should revert to a thoughtful interaction with them about the biblical principles that address his or her wrong choices. As always, Christian parents must turn to fervent prayer that God the Holy Spirit would change their hearts, fill them, lead them, and guide them in their life choices. Remember, we pray for miracles.

So . . . what have we learned?

1. How is culture defined? What is the basic social unit?
2. Where should culture originate? Where does it originate today?
3. What is the cultural commandment?
4. What does the Proverb refer to when it speaks of "tying your

mother's commandments around your wrist?"

5.   What is the purpose of music according to Colossians 3:16? What is the purpose of music according to the worldview of Romanticism?

6.   What are the two critical elements required in our celebrations, according to Deuteronomy 16?

7.   What is the grand principle governing eating, drinking, and entertainment found in Romans 14?

8.   What are the three tests for making good entertainment choices?

9.   What are some of the balances mentioned that, if maintained, will help your family to avoid excessive immersion in entertainment?

So . . . how are we doing?

1.   How often does our family unplug the earphones and enjoy entertainment in community as a family? Do we watch videos together and then do we discuss them together as a family? Are we passive in our reception of media, or do we actively discern?

2.   How much gratitude does our family express to God in the following areas?
   - Meals
   - Movies and Music
   - Snacks
   - People and relationships
   - Vacations
   - God's creation
   - Gifts and talents given to the members of the family

3. How do we provide oversight of our younger children's involvement in entertainment? How does this change as our children grow older?

Resources:

- *The Tattooed Jesus: What Would the Real Jesus Do With Pop Culture?* by Kevin Swanson
- *Media Choices: Convictions or Compromise?* by Phillip Telfer
- *Captivated: Finding Freedom in a Media-Captive Culture* (Documentary)

8 FAMILY EDUCATION

Almost everybody would agree that education is important. A survey conducted by the Christian pollster George Barna found that twice as many born-again parents considered a good education as a more important parental emphasis than a meaningful relationship with Jesus Christ.[62] Education was by far the most important parental concern among Christian families surveyed.

First off, I define education as "preparation of a child intellectually, emotionally, physically, and spiritually for life and for eternity." As the child is considered as an integrated person complete with body and soul, emotions and mind; these elements of the whole person cannot be treated separately. Immediately, the reader will see that the definition of education is dependent upon one's worldview or one's basic view of reality. From a biblical perspective then, education is just another aspect of the discipleship of the child. The end game for this exercise of inculcating knowledge and wisdom is to show the way to walk (Prov. 2:9; 4:11,14,18, 26, 27). Simplicity, insobriety, and perpetual immaturity is not God's desire for the young man according to Proverbs 2:4 and Titus 2:6. Education prepares a man and a woman to know God, to fear God, and to show a pattern of good works (Prov. 2:5, Titus 2:7).

What then constitutes a "good education?" Given that education is important to the life of a child and to the future of the Church and human society, it seems that God might have something to say about it. A quick search in a Bible concordance reveals an entire book dedicated to the subject of imparting knowledge, wisdom, and understanding to a young man or a young woman (Prov. 1:1-6). The entire book of Proverbs chronicles a father's training of his son, with the addendum of the mother's instructions in the last chapter.

At this point in history, there is a strong tendency to ignore such wisdom, and most modern families do. They have a hard time believing that God would have anything to say about education or anything relevant to day-to-day life. They would sooner follow the ideas of Plato, Jean-Jacques Rousseau, Horace Mann, and John Dewey than they would God's Word. After all, these men are the "experts," and the architects of the greatest empires in the world. These are the two sides in the heart of the battle for the minds and the souls of the next generation.[63]

An increasingly secularized education system will always produce an increasingly secularized society. That should go without saying. If Christian influence in the culture has very much dissipated since 1900, it isn't for lack of Christian evangelism and Christian churches. Church attendance remains as high as ever. However, each successive generation is discipled in the schools by teachers who were discipled in secularized public or Christian universities. Following the generational trajectories, Pew Research finds that the Millennial generation is far more likely to be pro-homosexual, pro-evolution, and pro-socialist than the previous generation. [64]

Several years ago, I did a comprehensive study on what the greatest Christian pastors and teachers over the last two thousand years have said about education.[65] Across the board, throughout the centuries, these men of God warned parents against a secular education. Here are just a few examples of these warnings:

> Children are being taught perverse things in the schools. They hear them on the wireless and see them on television. The whole emphasis is anti-God, anti-Bible, and anti-supernatural. Who is going to counter these trends? That is precisely the business of parents.
> –Martyn Lloyd-Jones (1960s)

> Place the lives of children in their formative years, despite the convictions of their parents, under the intimate control of experts appointed by the state. . . where the mind is filled with the materialism of the day, and it is difficult to see how even the remnants of liberty can subsist. Such a tyranny, supported as it is by a perverse technique used as the instrument in destroying human souls is certainly far more dangerous than the crude tyrannies of the past.
> –J. Gresham Machen, founder of the Orthodox Presbyterian Church (1920s)

> I am as sure as I am of Christ's reign that a comprehensive and centralized system of national education, separated from religion, as is now commonly proposed, will prove the most appalling enginery for the propagation of anti-Christian and atheistic unbelief, and of anti-social nihilistic ethics, individual, social and political, which this sin-rent world has never seen.
> –A.A. Hodge, Presbyterian President of Princeton University (1880s)

For what end do you send your children to school? 'Why, that they may be fit to live in the world?' In which world do you mean—this or the next?...To send them to school (permit me to speak plainly) is little better than sending them to the devil. At all events, then, send your boys if you have any concern for their souls, not to any of the public schools (for they are nurseries of all manner of wickedness).
–John Wesley, Founder of the Methodists (1760s)

I am much afraid that the universities will prove to be the great gates of hell, unless they diligently labor in explaining the Holy Scriptures, and engraving them in the hearts of youth. I advise no one to place his child where the Scriptures do not reign paramount. Every institution in which men are not unceasingly occupied with the Word of God must become corrupt.
–Martin Luther, Founder of the Lutheran Church (1540s).

Well did the Apostle Paul warn concerning Greek learning with these words, "Beware lest any man spoil you through philosophy and vain deceit" (Col. 2:8). He draws a sharp contrast between the wisdom of the Greeks (1 Cor. 1:22) and Christ who is the wisdom of God (1 Cor. 1:24). He refuses to speak of the wisdom of this world and of the princes of this world (1 Cor. 2:6), which he says is sure to come to nothing. With these words, Paul claims the entire structure of Greek wisdom and humanist knowledge to be wrong, and all of their categories of thought are misconceived. What is this Greek wisdom, but that system of thought organized by Aristotle, Plato, and Socrates?

Most church denominations have gone into retrograde or apostasy because each successive generation is taught in humanist schools, universities, and seminaries. Parents and pastors alike assume that education is neutral. After all, we don't confine ourselves to purchasing "Christian" gas for our vehicles. So then why would we want to insist upon "Christian" education for our children? However, ideas are not neutral. Every approach to knowledge is set on a certain presuppositional worldview framework. Every textbook and every teacher in every classroom holds to some basic understanding concerning the nature of reality, truth, and ethics. After spending 10,000 hours in these classrooms, of course children will be affected by what they hear.

What Did God Say?

The Book of Proverbs provides the basic constituents of God's wisdom and His approach to education:

1. Parents are important. The Bible assigns the responsibility of raising children to parents (Deut. 6:7, Eph. 6:1-4, Col. 3:20-21, 1 Thess. 2:11, the entire book of Proverbs) While delegation of some of the tasks in the discipleship of children is not out of the question, especially when it comes to specific skill areas, parental involvement is normative in Scripture. The secular world dismisses parents quickly, but we don't find this in the wisdom of Scripture. When God assigns a responsibility to the sphere of family, we had better not allow the traditions of men to relieve the family of that responsibility in any way (Matt. 15:4-6). Our Lord levels a severe condemnation upon the Pharisees for doing this very thing with their system of Corban.

2. Education will always serve the purposes of the family economy or family discipleship. It is therefore, a function of the family. We are interested in both forming our children's character and their skills. The school has no other purpose than to train a child in faith, character, and life skills. Should we provide training for a child in engineering or nursing for example, it would be for the purpose of supplementing a family economy. If we want to teach them about

the liberal arts, to include epistemology (the nature of truth), reality (both natural and supernatural), and ethics (that which is right and wrong), we would never want them to take this apart from faith in God, God's truth, God's worship, and God's ethical commands. This is clearly discipleship. Wherever humanists introduce a third category of knowledge separated from life and faith into the Christian school, the Christian theory of education is compromised.

3. One-on-one catechetical instruction is the default method to be used in the discipleship of our children (Ex. 13:8,14, Deut. 6:20). Most educators understand the power of one-on-one mentorship or tutorship, but we find it particularly important if the child's character and faith is the primary interest of the teacher. I recommend one-on-one instruction when 1) the most important lessons of life are being inculcated, 2) new material is being introduced for the very first time, and 3) a child's progress in the material is stymied somehow. Large classrooms simply cannot provide this level of attention, and hardly any child will learn how to read well, without every-day, one-on-one tutorship for one to two years.

4. Christian education respects the principle of individuality (1 Cor. 12:4-12, Song of Songs 8:8-12). The principle of individuality embraces the differences in our children's learning styles, gifts, and abilities. In the wisdom of God, He did not make any two children exactly alike.

However, the modern state has greatly abridged Christian liberty by imposing a certain education regimen on every child. It is a form of tyranny, and the damage done to education over the last hundred years has been disastrous. Modern socialist systems with their one-size-fits-all approach cannot tailor-make an educational experience for each child. These huge centralized-and-standardized government programs will mass produce education, processing children like widgets through a manufacturing center. Some may fit well in the mechanical process and they will make good citizen workers, efficient cogs in the gigantic mechanism of a government-run economy. Children are not widgets, however. They come in many shapes and sizes, equipped with a wide variety of gifts and abilities. Every child responds differently to various teaching methods. They have varying learning styles. They learn at a thousand different rates. There is no way that the centralized state can guarantee a well-educated populace. Nobody knows children better than their own parents, and therefore parental decision-making relating to education is of the highest importance.

Throughout their K-12 years, my children never knew their "grade level." They progressed at their own speed in math, science, and reading. We maximized on their gifts and challenged them in their weak areas. We provided creative coursework that would supplement their abilities and interest areas.

5. Faith and character should be preeminent in the teaching process. Since the Book of Proverbs is the source book on the education of a child, then why is there so little to be found of geography, geology, and geometry in it? Why would God permit such a "gross oversight" in this important book on education? If we are to assume that God knew what He was doing when He wrote the book of Proverbs, then there must be a reason why He would choose not to emphasize certain material. The facts of geography, geology, and geometry must not be as essential in the education of a child.

If the education of a child can be seen as a building, faith and character is the concrete foundation, the structure, the studs, and the drywall. Geography, geometry, and geology provide the wallpapering. Of course, it is the wallpaper that makes the house beautiful. But if it were not for the structure, where would we hang the wallpaper? The Book of Proverbs addresses human relationships, the theory of knowledge, ethics, psychology, conflict resolution, economics, and political leadership. However, the wisdom of God does not separate the raw facts about these specific areas of knowledge from character, morality, and life.

While I was homeschooling my son, he was always a year or two ahead in mathematics. At one point, however, it seemed that he was not applying his full potential to the material. So I challenged him with a test of character. If he could not achieve 85% on the unit test, he would have to go back over the entire unit again. When he failed to make the mark, of course he was disappointed. He said he had a good grasp of the material, so why should he have to do the unit all over again? I reminded him that we were not really teaching mathematics here; we were teaching character. We were just using math as a convenient means for teaching the character trait of diligence. This is the focal point of the Christian parent.

6. Our children should be able to read and copy out the Word of God. This is the plain teaching of Deuteronomy 6:8-9 and this has been the basis for all education in the Western Christian world.

> "You shall teach them diligently to your sons and shall talk of them when you sit in your house and when you walk by the way and when you lie down and when you rise up. You shall bind them as a sign on your hand and they shall be as frontals on your forehead. You shall write them on the doorposts of your house and on your gates." (Deut. 6:7-9)

In the more primitive home of the Jewish family, there was not much accessibility to paper. Walls and doors served as the most accessible flat surfaces in public view. The expectation maintained in the Jewish and Christian homes is that children would be able to read the Word of God on the walls and anywhere they would find it. This key objective was the basis for the first law addressing education in the American colonies —"The Old Deluder Satan Act" of 1647.

> It being one chief project of that old deluder, Satan, to keep men from the knowledge of the Scriptures… it is therefore ordered that every township in this jurisdiction, after the Lord hath increased them to fifty households shall forthwith appoint one within their town to teach all such children as shall resort to him to write and read, whose wages shall be paid either by the parents or masters of such children.

In general, therefore, our children should be trained to read and write well enough to be able to read a Bible that reflects a good translation from the Greek and Hebrew manuscripts. By the time they are eight or nine years old, we can expect them to read fluidly out loud, without much correction. Naturally, there will be exceptions to the rule. Some children begin reading at three and some will begin reading at eight or nine and then usually learn at a more accelerated rate.

7. The fear of God is the most basic principle, and the first mentioned in God's book on education.

> "The fear of the LORD is the beginning of knowledge: but fools despise wisdom and instruction." (Prov. 1:7)

There is no more important principle underlying the Christian view of knowledge than this. Fundamentally, we would not seek out a Christian homeschool curriculum or Christian school merely to teach "creation" vs. "evolution." We are not thinking of a Bible class tacked on to the school day. We want to teach biology, chemistry, physics, math, literature, and history in *the fear of God*. We cannot teach apologetics or argue for the existence of God without assuming the very foundational principle of all of human knowledge—the fear of God. Sexual education in the fear of sexually transmitted diseases is a waste of time, as most Christian conservatives discovered in the 2000s. Where there is no fear of God before their eyes, the sexual revolution will continue unabated.

Worship must be carefully integrated into science and history classes. Awe and reverence for God is something that must be cultivated. Effective teachers and disciplers will be more interested in students learning the fear of God in their chemistry classes than students learning chemistry. This element alone will yield a radically different form of education.

Several years ago, my wife found a dead raccoon on the side of the road, still in pretty good shape. She brought the animal home and stored it in the freezer for future use in her biology class. When the day arrived for the dissection, the local homeschool group gathered and knives were poised to cut into the animal. Before commencing the dissection, we took a moment to admire the creation of almighty God, and we offered up prayers of praise and thanksgiving to Him for this awesome creature. This is the most important part of the biology laboratory, and rarely do colleges train young people in reverence, awe, wonder, and fear.

With scanning electron microscopes and powerful telescopes available to him, 21st century man has a thousand times more knowledge of the magnitude and complexity of this universe than the 18th century scientist. What we know about the human cell is far more complete today—this biological building block is more complex than a Boeing 747 assembly plant! To fail to give glory to God for His awesome creation (while giving glory to man for his limited knowledge of God's creation), is nothing short of cosmic treachery. What will science sans the fear of God do to itself throughout the generations? I tremble to think of how modern man is already poised to destroy himself through weapons of mass destruction, genetic engineering, stem cell research, cloning, immunizations drawn from fetal tissue, and environmental science. After a century or two of secular education (where the fear of God is banned in public school classrooms), what will happen to these empires?

Whenever history, science or literature is taught, fundamental perspectives are always conveyed through the textbooks and teachers. The fundamental perspective is called a "worldview." If God, church, prayer, and Christ are not mentioned in the child's readers over a period of five years of primary school work, then the message is clear: *God, church, prayer, and Christ are not important*. If God's providence is not mentioned as the key causal factor in history, then the message is clear: *History is the product of random chance and man's "sovereign" will*. Always a worldview is conveyed. Sadly, millions of Christian families around the world have been deceived to think that education provided by the humanists and the Greeks is just a neutral thing. Their children are given the wrong worldview (or religious perspective) in the schools and more often than not, they will abandon their parent's faith. This has been the legacy of the entire post-Christian world for many generations.

8. Life application is probably the most powerful principle in a Christian theory of education. Most education is a waste of time because there is so little relevance to it, and hence there is little retention. The student misses the relevance entirely because there is no application of the knowledge he received.

> "Be you doers of the word, and not hearers only, deceiving your own selves. For if any be a hearer of the word, and not a doer, he is like unto a man beholding his natural face in a mirror: for he beholds himself, and goes his way, and immediately forgets what manner of man he was." (James 1:22-24)

This is the Christian theory of knowledge, very different from that of the humanist and Greek wisdom (1 Cor. 1:22-23). Knowledge puffs up (1 Cor. 8:1), but serving others in love keeps us humble. There is nothing more humbling than attempting an application of the knowledge we have received, because we realize our limitations in the application. It is in the application that we make our mistakes.

Actually, James 1 teaches that knowledge is incomplete and transient without application.

Much of education ignores this application, and so knowledge comes across as irrelevant and useless to the life of the student. This is why some say that "A" students end up teaching, and "B" students end up working for "C" students. When education is put on an island of academia (apart from family, business, politics, and church), it becomes sterile and isolated from life. Suppose we learned to ride a bicycle by taking Bike 101, Bike 102, Bike 103, Bike Statics, Bike Dynamics, and Bike Accident Recovery Workshop over a period of twelve years. Since we never quite mounted the bicycle through many years of study, the material would come across as theoretical, meaningless, irrelevant, and boring. The same applies to writing, reading, mathematics, science, and history.

Education is not merely the pressing of isolated facts into the mind of a student. Education is discipleship in which knowledge is conveyed and integrated into life. The student must learn the "facts," but the teacher is not satisfied until the student knows how the facts are relevant to some life application.

9. Relationships form the heart of learning and discipleship. At a key moment in the Book of Proverbs, the father cries out to his son:

> "My son, give me your heart, and let your eyes observe my ways." (Prov. 23:26)

This is not the kind of statement you will hear from your college calculus prof, because relationships are not important in the sterile academic environment. I never had a college professor confront me about pride, or sexual sin, or anything else. Modern educators are seldom reminded of their role to disciple their students. They are given the impression that their only responsibility is to stuff facts into the brains of pupils gathered in the room. I once heard of a seminary professor who gave a lesson on practical theology and he told his students, "These congregants are not your friends. If you want a friend, get a dog." Clearly, this seminary professor was not Jesus, because Jesus called His disciples "friends," and then He said, "Greater love hath no man than this, that a man lay down his life for his friends" (John 15:13).

Children are not widgets, and they are not computer hard drives into which we stuff a string of facts. They are human beings with personalities, and they are made in the image of God. This truth should change the way we look at education! Human beings respond best to relationship. They respond best to love.

The modern school of course does not allow for corporeal punishment done in love and it does not allow for hugs and kisses either for fear of sexual perversion. As parents communicate love for their children in the context of family-based education, this love really does transcend many problems in the academic realm.

10. The Christian parent should be equally concerned with the medium of communication and the content communicated in literature, art, music, theater, and all of the liberal arts. Christian liberal arts teachers have said that all well-written literature is good literature. They hold that literature created by the great humanists, the Greeks, the transcendentalists, and the Unitarians ought to be studied rather uncritically in the Christian classroom. After all, these are the great masters and we ought to set our children at their feet for years in order that they may study their content and method. If the content is flawed, at least the writing is pure genius and ought to be copied, they say. However, they forget the wisdom of Proverbs 21:4.

> "A haughty look, a proud heart, and the plowing of the wicked, is sin." (Prov. 21:4)

If the plowing of the wicked is sin, so is his rhetoric. The innuendoes in his writing, the haughty sarcasm, the humorous turn of the phrase, his choice of words, and his proud heart—all of it is sin.

The devil is a good writer. He may be among the best masters of rhetoric in the created universe. His best work may have been providing great curriculum for Christian schools over the centuries.

Several years ago, I taught rhetoric at a local classical Christian school using the assigned text, which was Aristotle's *Rhetoric*. From the outset, I highlighted 1 Peter 3:15 as the core biblical verse that sets the stage for all of Christian rhetoric:

> "But sanctify the Lord God in your hearts: and be ready always to give an answer to every man that asks you a reason of the hope that is in you with meekness and fear." (1 Pet. 3:15)

It is only a single verse, with only two words dedicated to method in rhetoric—meekness and fear. I took these character traits to be important: in fact, highly critical. However, I searched in vain for a single mention of these virtues in Aristotle's *Rhetoric*. In this philosopher's treatment of *Ethics*, he is careful to make the point that "modesty is not a virtue" and boasting is commended if it is used to "win fame and honor."[66] This is a fatal mistake to be found in all humanist education, and this method means death to their empires. But then again, what do fishermen know about rhetoric?

Perhaps the greatest curse that has ever befallen Christian families comes when they give their children an education that is lacking in Christ's humility and the fear of Almighty God. The great humanists and unbelieving literary giants know nothing of this, and therefore their greatest works turn into the greatest folly and danger for Christian children. Well did Martin Luther say of Aristotle, "If Aristotle had not lived in the flesh, I should not hesitate to call him a devil."[67]

The curriculum we provide our children in the early years should focus primarily on Scripture. This is the core curriculum required by God Himself (Deut. 6:7). As our children better understand the Scriptures, I recommend next adding in the best books (the classics) written by Christians. Give them the best teachers or the best writers in history; those who have retained a Christian way of thinking in method and content. Finally, as our children approach their senior year in high school, they may begin to read the "great" literature written by influential unbelievers who presented a liberal arts philosophy built up on human reason and humanist presuppositions. By this time, when they read these unbelieving perspectives they ought to be well-prepared to critique the worldviews that counter a biblical way of thinking, because of the solid foundation that was laid earlier in their education.[68]

Christ the Center

The three most important events in all of human reality are the creation, the cross, and the final judgment. The key Person involved in all three events is the Son of God. The Lord Jesus Christ is the center of human history, and His incarnation became the great interruption in human existence. Therefore, no field of study in this world should ever ignore Christ, for truly He is the "elephant in the room" of knowledge.

> "For by him were all things created, that are in heaven, and that are in earth, visible and invisible, whether they be thrones, or dominions, or principalities, or powers: all things were created by Him, and for Him: and He is before all things, and by Him all things are held together." (Col. 1:17)

The Son of God himself is the Genius who conceptualized and formed every physical thing, every physical law, and every physical order in the universe. By His power, He holds together every atom, every physical process, every eco system, every social system, and every political state. He controls the rate of thermodynamic decay, and assures the conservation of energy. He sovereignly ordains the progression of every germ, bacterium, and virus on earth.

Christ is above all thrones and dominions, and He should be of central importance in the civics classroom as well. His hands are on every historical event. His kingdom is all that really matters. Generally, most history classes thoroughly cover the kingdoms of men, but the kingdom of Jesus Christ and His church are ignored or even derided. If He is "head over all things to the church," it is a supreme dishonor to ignore Jesus Christ in any field of study, given His importance to history, science, origins, redemption, and all of human behavior.

He was in the beginning with the Father, and then He was born of a virgin in a stable in Bethlehem right around 0 A.D. As Jesus was introduced at His baptism and at His transfiguration, it seems that God the Father was interested in one thing— that everyone listen to Him (Matt. 17:5). Now, God has spoken to us by His Son (Heb. 1:3), and any who refuses to listen to Him now will receive the most horrible judgment possible (Heb. 12:25-26). He introduces Himself as "the Truth" itself (John 14:6), and it would be a travesty to ignore this Truth in the education of a child.

Writing on the importance of Darwin in education, John Dewey (the father of modern public education) called God "a faded piece of metaphysical goods." In his article written in 1910, this father of the modern public schools declared an end of 2,000 years of the "fixed and the final," clearly alluding to Jesus Christ and His influence upon Western thought. We disagree. Christ is still the center of our reality, our history, our lives, and our knowledge, and that is the way it will be in our children's education.

Higher Education

The principles of a good education remain the same for the twenty-something as for the eight-year-old. Proper discipleship will take into account the whole person, spiritual and academic. Every young person will need a careful combination of books, spiritual account-ability and worship, and life integration in their preparation for life. Most colleges provide books, but very little, if any, life integration and daily spiritual accountability. For these reasons, I recommend mentorship as a great way to incorporate more spiritual accountabil-ity and life integration into the mix. One option is to have a young person retain spiritual accountability in his home, while using an online college program for his education in the books. College min-istries have offered some spiritual accountability, but real life appli-cation in the work world is seldom part of the college experience.

In a day when college expenses are higher than ever, college debt is spiraling out of control,[69] unemployment for youth is on the rise,[70] and only 27% of college graduates have a job associated with their field of study,[71] this is no time to just accept the status quo. There is much potential for making wasteful decisions that will negatively affect our children's lives. Most colleges present the wrong world-view and the wrong social view, very much opposed to the biblical world and life view. As already pointed out, education has been the primary means of producing the generational apostasy that is so common today. Families need to come up with "out of the box" solu-tions that provide solid spiritual and academic preparation for their young sons and daughters. Make no mistake about it, the souls and the lives of our children are at stake.

So. . . what have we learned?

1. How does the author define education?
2. What book in the Bible is dedicated to the topic of education?
3. How does the modern totalitarian state run against the prin-ciple of individuality?
4. What is preeminent in the education of a child, according to the Book of Proverbs?
5. What is essential to the impartation of knowledge according

to James 1:22-24?

6. What is the foundational building block of knowledge, according to Proverbs 1:7?

7. What was the main concern of the "Old Deluder Satan Act?"

8. How do Peter and Aristotle differ on the subject of rhetoric?

9. What sequence does this chapter recommend for teaching literature?

10. What combination of three elements does the author recommend for the preparation of the post high-school student?

11. Why is it important that Christ remain at the center of the curriculum and teaching in your child's education?

So. . . how are we doing?

1. Which of the ten principles outlined in this chapter is most lacking in modern education, in your view? Which of these ten principles have you tended to overlook in your children's education?

2. What are the strengths and/or the dangers of the education recommended by Aristotle?

3. As parents, what are your highest goals and commitments for your children?

More Resources:

- *Upgrade: The Ten Secrets to the Best Education for Your Child* by Kevin Swanson (available from generations.org)

- *Keep the Faith: On Education, edited* by Kevin Swanson (available from generations.org)

- *Great Christian Classics Curriculum* (available from generations.org)

- *Kickstart: Launch Your Life* (video sessions and workbook, available from generations.org)

9 FAMILY, CHURCH, & STATE

It is hoped that this book has provided a simple synopsis of the biblical content on the family, staying as close to Scripture as possible. How often have the traditions of men distracted us away from the law of God, as Jesus put it in Matthew 15:6? Every generation or two, we need to question the traditions of men by a careful reassessment of the principles God has given us, especially as pertaining to the relationship of family, Church, and state.

The Church in our day has very much failed to support the biblical vision of the integrated family. On a visit with relatives in another city a number of years ago, we attended a large evangelical church on Sunday, all five of our children in tow. As we sat down in a pew towards the front, we were notified by an usher that our children were not welcome in the worship service. Apparently, the children's program running concurrently with the worship service was not optional. After a little polite discussion, the ushers finally directed us to the back of the church where we sat together through the service. It has only been in the last thirty years that children have been removed from the worship services in many, if not most, of the larger churches in this country.

Churches began offering Sunday Schools for street children and orphan children in the latter part of the 18th century. Concomitant with the disintegration of family life in the 20th century came a host of church programs designed for the children and for the rising social group called "adolescents." During the 1980s and 1990s, "children's church" became the fashion as an alternative to the regular worship service. Truly these were revolutionary changes attending the seismic social shifts of the day.

Where the culture clashes with Scripture, modern expositors are tempted to back away from the altercation. They do not like to see the Church engage "contra mundum" (against the world.) So, the Church passively accepts the disintegrated family model and simply accommodates it. Why force the issue when world's entire social system is geared differently? It would be much easier to contextualize the Church so as to be relevant to the culture surrounding us. What these folks forget is that the world is in a death spiral and their sexual and social systems are part of the problem. Our Lord Jesus Christ came to call sinners to repent of this wrong-headed and sinful approach to family life (as well as other relevant sins).

The Church above all should lead in this reformation of family life, especially as the Church relates to the family. In the Old Testament, foreigners who wanted to partake of the Passover (and thereby join in with the "wilderness church") would have all of their sons circumcised (Ex. 12:48). There are no examples of baptisms of individual children from Christian homes in the New Testament, nor do we find professions of faith made by anybody but adults. However, we do find entire households baptized together in the New Testament, and children who were of sufficient age to understand what they were saying would join the public professions in the Old Testament (Neh. 10:28-29). We also find many examples of children integrated into the public assembly throughout the Bible (Deut. 16:9-14; 32:46; Josh. 8:34-35; 2 Chron. 20:13; Ezra 10:1; Neh. 8:2; 12:43; Joel 2:15-16; Matt. 19:14, Acts 20:7-12). There are instances throughout Scripture where the elders meet together (Acts 15) and where the assembled crowd seems to have been exclusively men (Acts 2). Yet, the core assembly of the church included the integrated families. Children are not excluded. When the church gathered to hear the Apostle's doctrine read at Ephesus and Colossae, the children are addressed (Eph. 6:1-4, Col. 3:20). They were accepted as saints (1 Cor. 7:14, cf. 1 Cor. 1:2).

The Traditions of Men

We ought always to be sensitive to any repetition of the problem Christ outlined in Matthew 15:5-6. How have we made the commandment of God of none effect by our traditions? While I would not condemn any particular church program, each parent and each pastor should ask themselves this question. The Lord our God has uniquely equipped and empowered Christian parents to provide discipleship for their children as they sit in their homes (Deut. 6:7). He wants fathers to bring their children up in the nurture and the admonition of the Lord (Eph. 6:4). If human institutions (including churches) have by the aggregate of their programs displaced God's commandments in the minds of the parents of the church, then something ought to be done about it. Something ought to be said about it.

Paul's youth programs as outlined in Ephesians 6 were remarkably simple. Addressing the fathers, he told them to bring their children up in the nurture of the Lord. Then, turning to the children, he said, "Honor him. Listen to him. Obey him." What would happen if the church would put a little impetus behind this "program?" What if the church would empower, encourage, and equip parents to that task? Would we see the 40% apostasy rate in Christian homes that we see today? Eighty percent of Millennials were raised in Christian homes, but only 56% call themselves Christians today.[72] Fewer attend church. Only 0.5% of Mosaics hold to a biblical worldview, down from 14% percent among their parent's generation.[73] That accounts for a 97% retrograde rate in faith commitment within a single generation! There has never been an era where the church has poured so many resources into its youth and experienced such an extraordinarily high rate of apostasy. To say the least, the return on investment has been a disaster of unprecedented proportions.

The question thus remains for any parent or pastor who might give an honest answer: Are there any ways in which the traditions of men have made Deuteronomy 6:7 and Ephesians 6:4 of none effect? Have churches crossed the jurisdictional boundaries of the family at any point? Are fathers and mothers discouraged from their God-given authority and responsibilities in the raising of their children?

Even as we answer these questions, we must keep in mind that the church is still responsible for the spiritual care of the family and the children. Certainly, pastors and shepherds in the church should be vitally interested in the spiritual condition of the children in the church. Are they being taught the Word of God? Historically, the church has conducted catechism classes in which children were tested in their knowledge of the Word. The assumption, of course, was that families were doing the bulk of the discipleship work from Monday through Saturday. If families neglected this work, there wasn't much that a brief training class on Sunday could do to compensate for that.

Considering Our Children as God Considers Them

As Christian families and a Christian church, we must think of our children in biblical terms, using biblical terminology Not many churches still uphold these terms, but serious families who want to reform their families by the Word of God will do so.

Children raised in a home with at least one Christian parent are referred to as "holy" or "saints" in 1 Corinthians 7:14.

Children raised in the Christian church are considered "godly seed" in Malachi 2:15.

Children (even small babies) raised in the Christian church are considered "God's children" in Ezekiel 16:21.

Christian parents, do you refer to your children as holy ones, godly seed, and God's children? It takes faith to use terms like these for your children, because this language is God's language. Some theological systems would never permit such terms. We lose the terminology, because we really aren't thinking biblically. But Jesus said of little children and nursing babies, "Of such is the kingdom of heaven." Therefore, children should be considered members of the visible local church. They play an important role in the local body. When children cry out in our church service, I like to remind our congregants that it is "out of the mouths of babes and sucklings God has ordained strength because of the enemy" (Ps. 8:2).

How Do Our Children Get Saved?

This may be the most important question all Christian parents can ask. We come back to it again and again. How do children get saved? The simple answer is that God must save them, by the work of the Holy Spirit based in the accomplished work of the Son of God on the cross. Nonetheless, God has also assigned means by which the work is applied to our children. Parental discipleship is important, because it is commanded. However, there is something even more important to the salvation of our children, dare I say it. It is not Sunday school, Children's Church Fun and Games, or youth programs. It is the preaching of the Word of God.

> "How then shall they call on Him in whom they have not believed? And how shall they believe in Him of whom they have not heard? And how shall they hear without a preacher? And how shall they preach unless they are sent? As it is written: 'How beautiful are the feet of those who preach the gospel of peace, who bring glad tidings of good things!'" (Rom. 10:14-15)

These are the plain words of Scripture, and they apply as much to children as they do to adults. Our children must be taken to hear the Word of God proclaimed, preached, and heralded with authority, as an announcement from a king! It is through the "foolishness" of preaching (1 Cor. 1:18-27) that God chooses to work on the hearts of our children. Great pains should be taken by parents to attend to the preaching of the Word at least twice a week, perhaps even three or four times a week. The preacher may not necessarily be particularly eloquent or smooth in his delivery; however, if he takes the clear Word of God, verse by verse, and declares it with authority, explains it with clarity, and urges an application upon the congregation with fervency, all in dependence upon the Holy Spirit, then that is good enough for your family.

Baptism and the Lord's Supper

There is much controversy on this matter of when children may partake of these two ordinances of the church, and I have no interest in working it out in this short book (as if I could thereby resolve 2,000 years of controversy once and for all). Nevertheless, I will make just a few plain and simple points.

Baptism and the Lord's Supper are ordinances of the Church and enable communion in the body of Christ. They are relational sacraments. What a shame that the ordinances intended for unity of the body have become the basis of much of the disunity in the Church!

There are no instances of individual teens or children from Christian homes professing faith and being baptized in the Bible, or in the first few centuries of the Church. We do find examples of household baptisms, however.

As our children are baptized and take the Lord's Supper, they are invited into communion and fellowship in the church body. The Lord's Supper is called communion, *koinonia*, in 1 Corinthians 10:16-17. Children get the sense of "belonging" in the Church body as we participate in these ordinances together.

Our communion and union is with the Lord Jesus and with the rest of His body, the Church (1 Cor. 11:29, 12:13), so there is both a vertical and a horizontal aspect to these ordinances. In other words, the Lord's Supper is not just a "Me and Jesus" moment, because there is this body of believers around us that compose this communion.

Sticking with the Church

Sadly, many professing Christian families have walked away from the organized Church. Over the last forty-five years of my involvement in the homeschooling movement, I have seen this generational apostasy develop. It is a rather significant percentage of the movement. Their reasons vary: sometimes, it is disillusionment with the other sinners (worldliness and lack of orthodoxy at points), or unresolved personal conflicts. For many families, excessive church-hopping and complete rejection of church involvement becomes the road to apostasy. This describes much of the breach of faith over the last thirty years, in America especially. It is extremely dangerous. I can give no comfort to Christian families who have abandoned the

Church. Families have the impression that they can maintain the faith in their family without the Church for generations, but this is not true.

Jesus Christ came to build His Church, not just a few isolated "godly" families. However, godly churches are built with godly families, and the one contributes to the other. Strong families make for strong churches, and strong churches make for strong families. The Lord wants a church with healthy elders that substantially meet the guidelines in 1 Timothy 3:1-8, and a church where there is faithful discipline for gross sin (such as incest—1 Cor. 5), and where brothers and sisters confess their sins and love one another (1 John 1:8-9; 1 John 4:7-15). To those who say that they love God, but cannot stand being around God's kids, John says, "You don't love God." If you love God, you will love His children. There must be this basic attraction for every believer to the fellowship of the saints.

Involvement in the Local Church

The healthiest families I have ever seen are those who have been faithful to the church, come hell or high water. The gates of hell do not prevail. Somehow, they avoid the rifts in the church. They refuse to participate in the temporary schisms. They keep their heads down and serve the body following in the footsteps of the household of Stephanas, who were "addicted to the ministry of the saints" (1 Cor. 16:15). They participate joyfully in the preaching services and the prayer meetings. Only in a worst-case scenario when the church clearly abandons the Gospel or ordains homosexuals, will they leave the church to find another. We do not find these fathers continually arguing with the pastors over minor issues. Rather, they will ask intelligent questions and find edification in all of the preaching and "prophesying." They do not quench the Spirit by despising the gifts offered by others in the congregation (1 Thess. 5:19-20).

Although there are differences between families when it comes to certain applications of principles (relating to education, clothing, entertainment, etc.), humility must be the rule. The one who loves his brother will be concerned about not offending his brother, and he will be especially kind and careful in his handling of the weaker brother. The stronger brother does not whine about the weaker brother's weaknesses. He goes out of his way to avoid offending his brother by his dress, his food and drink choices, his medical advice, and so on. The stronger brother is strong because he is more humble, more sensitive of his sin, more thankful, and more given to worship than the weaker brother. He is not more licentious and sensual in his interactions with worldly entertainments. He is far less interested in the lust of the flesh, the lust of the eyes, and the pride of life. Rather, he is more thankful while he eats and drinks with his family. He worships God in every context, including the university chemistry classroom or the movie theater. While the weaker brother may not be so ready to fear God and worship Him in the chemistry classroom, the stronger brother will be more patient, more kind, and more loving towards the weaker brother, than the weaker brother is to him.

When "stronger" families leave churches because they can't put up with the weaker brothers, then we must conclude that they are not the stronger, but the weaker. When "stronger" churches with better doctrine have the least unity and the least love and meekness, they must be the weaker churches, in reality.

Instead of demanding church programs to satisfy their felt needs, the Christian family should be more occupied by serving and showing hospitality to strangers. Hebrews 13 provides these three basic admonitions to the church:

> "Let brotherly love continue. Do not forget to entertain strangers, for by so doing some have unwittingly entertained angels. Remember the prisoners as if chained with them—

those who are mistreated—since you yourselves are in the body also." (Heb. 13:1-3)

A church that follows these instructions avoids being the ingrown church or the clique-driven church. Healthy Christian families will find ways to love those who are close to them, and work through conflicts that inevitably arise in relationships. They will also look out for strangers, whether they are attending the church or just passing through the town. Perhaps the Christian family sets aside a special room to provide board for strangers. The dining room table will be well worn, and the guest book chock full of the names of those who have enjoyed hospitality in the home. Within the last hundred years, much of hospitality has become commercialized and people pay dearly to be treated well. Would Christians provide first class, warm service to strangers out of genuine love and expect nothing in return? Now that would present a powerful contrast to how the world does it.

Witnessing and Outreach

One of the concerns raised by Christian parents who are intent upon raising their children in the nurture of the Lord, is that they will isolate their children. On the one hand, we are called to "come out from among them and be separate" and "touch not the unclean thing" (2 Cor. 6:17). Our Lord Jesus Christ is severest in His criticisms of those who stumble their children. Certainly, parents must watch out for ungodly teachers, peers, entertainment, or cultural systems that would "offend one of the least of these little ones which believe" in Christ (Matt. 18:6).

On the other hand, the Lord calls us to "disciple the nations." We love our neighbor as ourselves. There isn't much encouragement on neighborhood evangelism in Scripture, but there is this neighbor love thing. Love for our neighbors will be manifested in neighborly kindness in word and deed. Thus, delivering cookies to neighbors, having them over for dinner, and picking up trash on the roadways is the day-to-day lifestyle of the Christian family.

While there is not very much on "witnessing" in Scripture, there is this all-important principle that characterizes the Christian life and the Christian family more than anything else:

> "A good man out of the good treasure of his heart brings forth good; and an evil man out of the evil treasure of his heart brings forth evil. For out of the abundance of the heart his mouth speaks." (Luke 6:45)

When our hearts are filled with gratefulness for God's forgiveness, Christ's sacrifice, deliverance from sin, and the hope of heaven, of course we are going to share it with somebody. It will not be a forced, mechanical thing. It will come as a natural outflow of the heart. As children observe their parents pouring out the abundant good treasure of their hearts with others, they will see that their parents' faith is real.

The other day we were visiting a small town on the West Coast. I was sitting in a coffee shop while two of my daughters took a walk through the shopping district. When I caught up with them an hour later, I found them talking to a young couple just off the public sidewalk. After another half an hour of sharing the Gospel, I asked the homeless couple if they had a Bible with them. They had none, so one of my daughters ran across the street to a Bible book store and picked up two copies for them. We prayed with them and bought them lunch. The story related to us by the young couple was dark and hopeless, but we were excited to share with them the blazing hope that burned within us. My daughter thanked me afterward for helping her navigate the conversation, in asking the right questions, and integrating Scripture in at certain points.

We do not want to send our children into a situation in which they are indoctrinated by a false faith, and they have little opportunity to share their faith. Nor do we want to leave them alone in a hostile environment, where we cannot be available to give them spiritual and physical support as they witness.

Whenever we take our faith to the streets, the abortion clinics, and the university classrooms, we will run into more sinners who need to hear the Gospel. These witnessing opportunities are faith-building experiences for our children. Increasingly, they will see the contrast between the world and Christ, and the need for Christ in our communities. While we don't particularly want our children in secular classrooms where others preach at them, we *would* like them to see the power of the Gospel actually saving souls and transforming lives. Jesus came to call sinners to repentance, and we want to follow in His footsteps.

The Family and the State

Governmental tyranny in previous centuries focused on the assembly of Christians who wanted to worship God. This was the impetus for the first migrations to America in the 17th century. Now, it seems that tyrants are less interested in dominating the sphere of the Church, as they are the sphere of the family. The family and the family-integrated economy represents a stronger threat to socialism and the all-encompassing state than does the average church in our day.

This erosion of the family under the coercive force of big government statism is almost unprecedented in the history of the world. It began with the 18th century philosopher Jean-Jacques Rousseau, who abandoned his own children on the steps of an orphanage as soon as they were born, and then proceeded to write a book on education for the modern state. Modern historian Will Durant explained his agenda: "Rousseau wanted a system of public instruction by the state. He prescribed many years with an unmarried tutor, who would withdraw the child as much as possible from parents and relatives."[74] Some fifty years after Rousseau, the Prussian philosopher Johann Fichte produced his landmark speech, "An Address to the German Nation," in which he recommended that children be turned over to the state and subjected to compulsory education. Fichte's point was that "through forced schooling, everyone would learn that work makes free and working for the State, even laying down one's life to its commands, was the greatest freedom of all."[75] Thus, children came to belong to the state in the mind of the modern socialists, and freedom was re-defined as slavery to the modern state.

The root of this thinking first appears in Plato's *Republic*: a world in which temporary sexual liaisons between men and women produced the children, and "no parent should know his child, and no child should know his parent."[76] Elsewhere, Plato declared that children "belong to the state rather than to their parents."[77] The powerful ideas of these Enlightenment philosophers profoundly affected all modern institutions, and changed modern civilization.

With the transfer of education to the state came the transfer of ideological training into the hands of the state. Both the responsibility and freedom for parents to educate their own children were now moved under the government's jurisdiction. This is where the Christian worldview clashes with the secular, as Scripture plainly places the education of children in the hands of their parents (Deut. 6:7, the Book of Proverbs, Eph. 6:4, 1 Thess. 2:11). Parental rights are deeply encoded into biblical law, and tyranny by definition will violate God's law in order to aggrandize the power of the state (Ex. 21:16-20, 22; 22:16, Num. 30:1-15, 1 Sam. 8:11,18). Regrettably, churches are afraid to teach the laws of God and thereby pave the way for tyranny in most of our Western countries.

The confiscation of children at the hands of the state is a mark of great tyranny and oppression. In the worst-case scenario, Herod and the Pharaoh killed the little children of the Jews, and Deuteronomy 28:32 describe the horrific conditions in which children are removed from their parents' homes. Also, 1 Samuel 8:11-15 defines tyrants as those kings who commandeer children and ruin family economies. "This will be the behavior of the king who will reign over you: He will take your sons and appoint them for his own chariots . . . he will take your daughters to be perfumers, cooks, and bakers. And he will take the best of your fields, your vineyards . . . he will take a tenth of your grain and your vintage, and give it to his officers and servants." Verse 18 continues, "and you will cry out in that day because of your king whom you have chosen for yourselves." Given enough time, powerful kings and governments will eventually destroy the family economy. To destroy the foundation of human society is a grave mistake, and these nations will eventually pay for it.

Over the last several years, both Germany and Sweden have outlawed home education and have virtually expunged every remnant of it from their nations. In England, the wide-sweeping Cinderella Law of 2014 carried a maximum ten year prison sentence for any harm to a child's intellectual or emotional development, opening every family to some level of prosecution at the hands of the state.[78] Scotland has also recently implemented a "state guardians" program that is dangerously reminiscent of Orwell's dystopia. Under the new program, parents will be reported to the state for trivial mistakes such as forgetting a medical appointment.[79]

Every year, millions of parents and children are hassled by truancy laws, compulsory attendance laws, child labor laws, curfew laws, spanking laws, and social services, based on anonymous tips—almost all notorious violations of family liberties as defined by the law of God. This extensive network of child protective service agencies did not exist in the 1960s. The basis of all these encroachments is not child welfare, but the assumption that children belong to the state. Year by year, this tyranny only weakens the family and strengthens the power of the state. For families who still value their children and family integrity, these tyrannical impositions have created inconvenience, expense, discouragement, and fear.

Where the Civil Magistrate Should Get Involved

Modern Christians are often given the impression that government power is unlimited, and that it would be some sort of treason to even suggest that these governments must be held in check by God's laws. However, this thinking transfers God's authority to man, which is the ultimate treason against heaven (Rom. 13:1). From a biblical perspective, the state does have a right to interfere with a family when there is serious physical abuse (Ex. 21:22-24), or sexual abuse (Lev. 18:7, 29; 20:11, 17). However, the state does not have the right to prosecute a family for an unclean house, insufficient discipleship, or the like. Without a clear understanding of biblical jurisdictional boundaries, governments will abuse their powers and parental freedoms will not survive. This is critical battle for the 21st-century Christian family.

Conclusion

We live in difficult times, where the collapse of the family coincides with the rise of the totalitarian state and the mass perversion of sexuality. The Christian family and church is at the weakest point in centuries.

The time has never been better for family reformation, indeed a biblical reformation. Yet, the problems are so all-pervasive and desperate, that nothing short of a supernatural miracle from above will save ourselves and our families in the present conditions. The problems we face are no different than what any nation has ever faced before the Gospel came by missionaries and evangelists. The only difference is that our nations are more complacent, and they think they have already received a gospel. However, the true Gospel will bring about a radical transformation and the world will know it when by the grace of God, we have planted gardens in the ashes of these burned-out cities and nations. What a marvelous testimony the Christian Church will provide to the world, where all semblance of social and sexual order has completely unraveled! Truly, "the world is passing away, and the lust of it; but he who does the will of God abides forever" (1 John 2:17). This maxim will be increasingly evident in the years to come.

To sum up a reformation agenda, here are some final encouragements and exhortations for our Christian families:

1. Root all of your thinking about family, sexuality, gender roles, and all of life in the Word of God. Return to the biblical principles again and again.

2. Return to the simple Gospel message over and over again. Remind one another that it is Jesus who saves us from our sins. Our salvation comes by the grace of God, not of works, lest any man should boast. Ask yourself every day: Are we living in the reality of the Gospel of Jesus Christ in this home?

3. Don't be afraid of being too radical when it comes to reinventing a Christ-centered, biblically-based education for your children.

4. Be aggressive when it comes to discerning and exposing ungodly ideas latent in modern entertainment and culture. Tear down imaginations that exalt themselves above the knowledge of God in Christ (2 Cor. 10:4-5). If you are not doing this, you are probably absorbing ungodly culture, and it is absorb-

ing you.

5. Love the Church, respect the elders of the church, and serve in the body. Remember that fervent, agonizing prayer and bold preaching empowered by the Spirit of God is the only hope for revival in family, Church, and society. Embrace prayer and preaching with all that is in you.

So . . . what have we learned?

1. What do we find families doing together as a unit in the Old and New Testaments?
2. What did Paul's ministry to children look like as briefly summarized in Ephesians 6:1-4?
3. In times past, why did the church use a catechism?
4. What terminology does the Bible use to describe children who are raised in Christian homes?
5. How do people get saved according to Romans 10:14-15?
6. With whom do we have communion when we take the Lord's Supper?
7. What are the three duties of church members found in Hebrews 13:1-3?
8. What are the two biblical principles (found in two Bible passages) that lead us to witness to our unbelieving neighbors?
9. How might the Church violate the jurisdiction of the family?
10. How might the state violate the jurisdiction of the family?
11. How might the family violate the jurisdiction of the Church?
12. On what occasions might the state legitimately prosecute the family for criminal behavior?

So . . . how are we doing?

1. How do you think of your children's spiritual status? Do you use the same language that Scripture uses for them?

2. How strong is your family's participation in the local church, in the following areas?
   - Listening to the preaching of the word one to three times per week
   - Sticking with a church and working through conflicts
   - Contributing to the church with your gifts, including hospitality
   - Outreach and evangelism
   - Prayer for and with the church
3. Do you sufficiently isolate your children from the world? Do you reach out to the world with the Gospel and do your children participate in this? What does this look like?

Suggested Resources

- Join a worldwide Christian hospitality network at www.CandleInTheWindow.com

Books on Church Involvement

- *What Is a Healthy Church Member?* by Thabiti M. Anyabwile
- *The Hospitality Commands* by Alexander Strauch
- *Practicing Hospitality: The Joy of Serving Others* by Pat Ennis and Lisa Tatlock

Books on Family and State

- *The Story of Freedom* by Kevin Swanson (available from Generations.org)

Appendix

THE GEN2 SURVEY

I have no greater joy than to hear that my children are walking in the truth. (3 John 4)

Hardly a day goes by in which we are not reminded by some major news source that the "atheist" and "unaffiliated" religious categories are growing among Millennials. The media speaks of the waning influence of Christians in the culture, betraying just a small degree of secret delight.

Meanwhile, those who are still hanging on to the faith are looking for some little piece of good news about the millennial generation. Parents who love Jesus Christ desire nothing more than to see their children walking in the truth. That is why Generations sponsored the Gen2 Survey between 2013 and 2015. Under the oversight of Dr. Brian Ray from the National Home Education Research Institute, we conducted a survey of the spiritual health of 10,000 Millennials who grew up in Christian homes (during the 1990s and 2000s). How are they doing now? Who will "keep the faith," in the next generation? And, more importantly what were the positive influences that seemed to produce some generational continuity? The survey considered the influences of educational methodology, parental relationship, church involvement, and culture, on the spiritual condition of the Millennials.

While we know that there is no "silver bullet" or magic formula that will guarantee the best upbringing for our kids, there are some environments that are better than others. For example, if you forget to water your plants, or if you water your plants with hydrochloric acid, most likely your plants will not survive. A decent environment is important for the outcome, while we realize that God is completely sovereign over the increase—whether in terms of crops or kids. (Also, we should note that correlation does not absolutely establish causation. Even so, it does give us a measure of wisdom and reason to explore certain alternate approaches).

The best wisdom comes from God's Word, and these sorts of surveys only substantiate what we would have taken from Deuteronomy 6:7 and Ephesians 6:4.

The Results of the Gen2 Survey

The most startling revelations taken from the Gen2 Survey pertained to education methodology. The indices considered on Charts A, B, and C were "Belief in God," "Perspective of Evolution & Creation," and "Sexual Abuse." The differences were stark. The input variable considers the number of years attending public, private, and homeschool, showing the level of commitment to each form of education. Increased commitments to public school (i.e. the longer a student was public-schooled), indicated a higher likelihood of belief in naturalistic evolution, a lower likelihood of belief in God, and a higher likelihood of having been sexually abused (by their own admission).

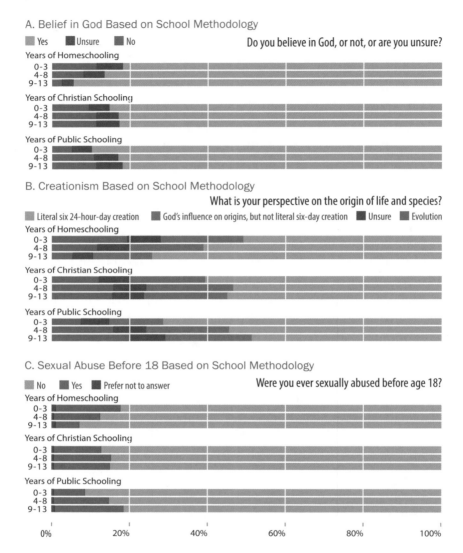

A. Belief in God Based on School Methodology

Do you believe in God, or not, or are you unsure?

B. Creationism Based on School Methodology

What is your perspective on the origin of life and species?

C. Sexual Abuse Before 18 Based on School Methodology

Were you ever sexually abused before age 18?

Surprisingly, Christian schooling yielded similar results to public schooling. However, homeschooling showed just the opposite trend – a much lower likelihood of belief in naturalistic evolution, a higher likelihood of belief in God, and a lower likelihood of being sexually abused. According to this study, the Christian-school student (spending 9-13 years in the institution) is 250% more likely to be sexually abused than the homeschool student (spending 9-13 years in homeschool). The public-school student (spending 9-13 years in public school) is 310% more likely to be sexually abused than the homeschooled student (spending 9-13 years being homeschooled). The Christian-school student is 270% more likely to believe in evolution than the homeschool student. The public school student is more likely to believe in evolution by a factor of 330%.

Of course, this does not mean that every Christian school is equally ineffective at producing students who uphold a biblical view of creation and believe in God, but the movement as a whole is called into question. The study compares the Christian school movement to the homeschool movement as a whole. This study looked at a wide

OUTPUTS in ADULT LIFE	Orthodoxy	Christian Behavior as Adults	Christian Beliefs as Adults	Satisfaction in Life as Adult	Civic/ Community Involvement	Beliefs Similar to Father's	Beliefs Similar to Mother's
Strong Relationship with Father	+++	+++	+++	+++	++	++++	++++
Strong Relationship with Mother	+++	+++	+++	+++	++	++++	++++
Attend Church at Early Age	+++	+++	+++	++	++	+++	+++
Attend Church at Older Age	+++	+++	+++	+++	++	+++	+++
Homeschool*	+++	+++	+++	++	♦	+++	+++
Christian School*	--	--	--	♦	++	--	--
Private School*	--	--	--	--	♦	--	--
Public School*	---	---	---	--	--	---	---

INPUTS into CHILD

* Compares those educated at least 7 years in their respective educational method.

distribution of the homeschool and Christian school populations. Generally, the study found negative results for the Christian school movement—at least, if the goal was to produce Christian believers, young people who exhibit Christian behavior, and hold to a biblical worldview. Chart D summarizes and compares the relative strength of correspondence between inputs and outputs.

Parental Relationships

The most telling set of charts produced by this study contrasted the homeschooled population with the general population in the area of parental relationship during the teenage years. The study considered a teen's relationships with both father and mother. Both were found to be equally important in the life of the teen. The father-teen relationship was no more important than the mother-teen relationship (and vice versa).

The output considered in the following charts was sexual activity outside of the covenant bond of marriage. What the Gen2 Survey produced is even more interesting. Referencing Chart E, the reader will note that solid father-teen relationships in the broader population (public-schooled and private-schooled students) contributed to a 60% better effect on sexual purity later in life. In other words, the father-child relationship is important to everybody's teenage years! However, Chart F addresses only the homeschooled population and here the improvement is much larger: 367%! This means that relationships within the homeschool context are six times more influential upon the life of a young person than those found in the general social context (attending conventional schools). Also, the homeschooled graduates who put the highest scores on their relationship with their father during the teen years maintained a 311% higher average score on sexual purity, than the broader population who testified to the same good relationship. Given that the homeschool context is closer to a 24/7 social setting, and peer contact is minimized (so it competes much less with the parental relationship), these numbers are not all that surprising.

The homeschool environment only provides a context in which a solid relationship between the child and the parents can occur and where other peer relationships are less important in the life of the

E. Average Millennial's Relationship with Father at age 16-17

Sexual encounter or physical relationship with someone outside of marriage?

 No ■ Yes

(Good relationship contributes 60% difference.)

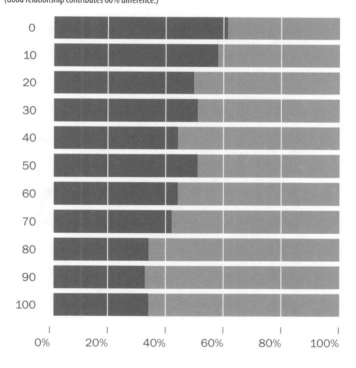

child. Obviously, there are homeschools in which the father-child or mother-child relationship is not good, and as would be expected, these generally do produce worse results (as determined by the outputs studied here). Incidentally, there was almost no difference between father-son relationships and father-daughter relationships on this metric.

F. Homeschool Millennial's Relationship with Father at age 16-17

Sexual encounter or physical relationship with someone outside of marriage?

 No ■ Yes

(Good relationship contributes 367% difference!)

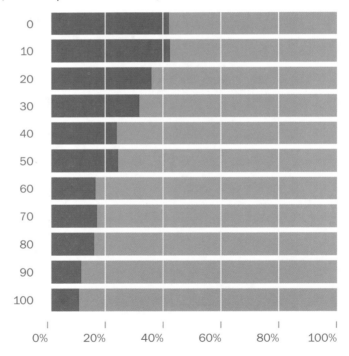

The Most Dramatic Chart

Chart G presents the most dramatic result of the entire study. This question examines the hypocrisy of the parents' lives, perceived by their children. Whether this question uncovered fundamental relationship difficulties or genuine hypocrisy cannot be discerned. However, it does appear that a parent's walk in accordance with his or her professed beliefs matters greatly in the raising of our children. Children who perceived their parents' hypocrisy did walk away from the faith. "Apostasy" refers to an entire abandonment of the Christian faith for atheism or agnosticism. The "apostate" was almost 600% more likely to refer to his parent's hypocrisy. Parents who do not walk the talk are sending another message home to their kids, and their kids are getting the message. Authenticity, humility, confession of sin, and true faith really matter, if the next generation is going to walk with God.

G. Parents' Influence and Example on Future Apostasy of Children

My parents' lives and actions make me more likely to adopt their religious standards and specific beliefs.

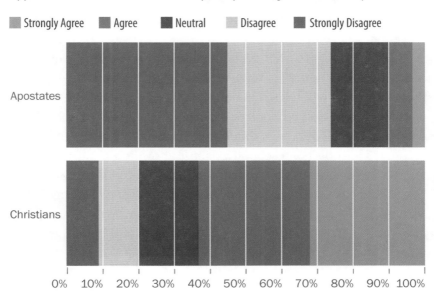

The Most Encouraging News

The question on the minds of most homeschool parents is: Will the first generation homeschool graduates homeschool their own children? Will they honor their parents' legacy in this way? Much sacrificial labor and resources have been spent building a movement outside of the $800 billion public school system. Much of this has been invested by parents who have wanted to see their children keep the faith, pass it on to their own children, and build the Kingdom of God through the generations. Here's the good news:

> 82% of homeschool graduates who were homeschooled for 7-12 years plan to use homeschooling for at least part of their children's education.

> 40% of graduates who were homeschooled 1-7 years plan to use homeschooling for at least part of their children's education.

There is a significant leap in commitment found with those home-schooled children that "made it the distance." Surviving the junior high and high school years appears to be very important if there is to be significant second-generation involvement in the homeschool movement.

This data suggests that second-generation growth in the home education movement is about to explode. Over the next fifteen years, these graduates will begin to homeschool their own children as second-generation homeschoolers. Assuming they will maintain the same average birth rate as the first generation (3.5 children), these graduates will be homeschooling about 5 million children by the year 2030. The homeschooling population in this country has grown by an average of a 6% per year increase for the last decade, and that is considered first generation growth. Extrapolating this 6% growth rate into the next fifteen years, we estimate a total homeschooling population for first and second generation homeschoolers will be ten million by 2030! Chart H shows the growth expected from both first- and second-generation homeschoolers over the next fifteen years.

H. Gen2 Growth of Homeschooling in the Next 15 Years

Assumptions

1. 60% growth (2003-2012) maintained
2. 82% of second generation continue to homeschool with 3.5 birth rate
3. Both Gen2 parents were homeschooled

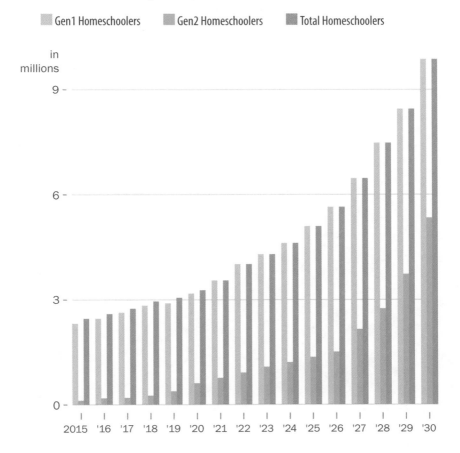

Gen1 Homeschoolers ▪ Gen2 Homeschoolers ▪ Total Homeschoolers

If you are a Christian living in America in the early part of the 21st century, I don't think you will find more interesting and encouraging news than this. While not all homeschoolers are Christians and homeschooling is no silver bullet, there is no question that it has produced some great fruit in an otherwise fairly ignoble time in human history. God has raised up a concerted minority that does not conform to the uniform humanist worldview taught by the public institutions. Will this fledgling movement make a difference for the faith, for the family, and for freedom in the years to come? Let us pray that God, by His grace, would bring about a great reformation of family life, family discipleship, family culture, family education, family relationships, and church life in this generation.

NOTES

1. "Gay, Lesbian and Straight Education Network," Wikipedia.org, https://en.wikipedia.org/wiki/Gay,_Lesbian_and_Straight_Education_Network
2. "Utah No. 1 in online porn subscriptions, report says," Deseret News, http://www.deseretnews.com/article/705288350/Utah-No-1-in-online-porn-subscriptions-report-says.html?pg=all
3. "Get the Latest Pornography Statistics," CovenantEyes.org, http://www.covenanteyes.com/2013/02/19/pornography-statistics/
4. see Paul Johnson, *Intellectuals: From Marx and Tolstoy to Sartre and Chomsky* (New York: Harper, 2007).
5. James Dobson, *Bringing up Boys* (Carol Stream: Tyndale, 2001), 121.
6. "Johns Hopkins: 57 Percent of Children Born to Millennials Are Out of Wedlock ," CNSNews.com, http://cnsnews.com/news/article/zoey-dimauro/johns-hopkins-57-percent-children-born-millennials-are-out-wedlock
7. John Blake, "Why young Christians aren't waiting anymore," http://religion.blogs.cnn.com/2011/09/27/why-young-christians-arent-waiting-anymore/comment-page-32/
8. Ibid.
9. see Al Mohler, *We Cannot Be Silent: Speaking Truth to a Culture Redefining Sex, Marriage, and the Very Meaning of Right and Wrong* (Nashville: Thomas Nelson, 2015), Rachel Ford, "Southern Baptist Leader: Birth Control is the "Sexual Misbehavior" That Led to Same-Sex Marriage," http://www.patheos.com/blogs/friendlyatheist/2015/12/19/southern-baptist-leader-birth-control-is-the-sexual-misbehavior-that-led-to-same-sex-marriage/
10. John MacArthur, "We Will Not Bow," http://www.gty.org/resources/sermons/80-425/we-will-not-bow
11. see Kevin Swanson, *Keep the Faith: On Family & Sexuality* (Parker: Generations, 2015). This book is available at generations.org.
12. "Contraceptive Use Is the Norm Among Religious Women," https://www.guttmacher.org/news-release/2011/contraceptive-use-norm-among-religious-women
13. see Kevin Swanson, *Keep the Faith: On Family & Sexuality*.
14. Ibid.
15. Bonnie Gayle, "I Didn't Have Kids Because They're Too Expensive — and I Have No Regrets," http://time.com/money/4082440/no-kids-too-expensive-no-regrets/
16. Dietrich Bonhoeffer, *Life Together: The Classic Exploration of Christian Community* (New York: HarperOne, 1954), 23-24.
17. Ibid., 28.
18. "U.S. Becoming Less Religious," http://www.pewforum.org/2015/11/03/u-s-public-becoming-less-religious/
19. Michael Lipka, "Millennials increasingly are driving growth of 'nones'," http://www.pewresearch.org/fact-tank/2015/05/12/millennials-increasingly-are-driving-growth-of-nones/

20. "Poll: Evangelical Millennials Support Homosexual Issues," http://www.christianheadlines.com/blog/poll-evangelical-millennials-support-homosexual-issues.html
21. see the summary of modern persecutions in Generations' upcoming publication, tentatively titled History of the Christian Church available at generations.org.
22. available at www.TheWorldview.com.
23. Dietrich Bonhoeffer, *Life Together: The Classic Exploration of Christian Community* (New York: HarperOne, 1954), 23.
24. George Barna, *Transforming Children Into Spiritual Champions* (Ventura: Regal, 2003), 125.
25. *Great Christian Classics: Five Remarkable Narratives of the Faith*, Ed. Kevin Swanson (Parker: Generations, 2013), 378.
26. Ibid., 370.
27. Benjamin Spock, *The Common Sense Book of Baby and Child Care* (1998), 215.
28. Joel Stein, "Millennials: The Me Me Me Generation," http://time.com/247/millennials-the-me-me-me-generation/
29. Elaine Jarvik, "Utah No. 1 in online porn subscriptions, report says," http://www.deseretnews.com/article/705288350/Utah-No-1-in-online-porn-subscriptions-report-says.html?pg=all
30. Wm. Paul Young, *The Shack: Where Tragedy Confronts Eternity* (Newbury Park: Windblown Media, 2008).
31. Jennifer G. Hickey, "Pew: Only 46 Percent of US Families Are 'Traditional'," http://www.newsmax.com/US/Family-single-parent-children-Pew-Research/2015/01/16/id/619047/
32. Jordan Weissmann, "For Millennials, Out-of-Wedlock Childbirth Is the Norm," http://www.slate.com/articles/business/moneybox/2014/06/for_millennials_out_of_wedlock_childbirth_is_the_norm_now_what.html
33. Audrey M. Jones, "Historical Divorce Rate Statistics," http://divorce.lovetoknow.com/Historical_Divorce_Rate_Statistics
34. Catherine Cloutier, "Most young Americans overwhelmingly support gay marriage," https://www.bostonglobe.com/news/nation/2015/06/26/almost-millennials-support-same-sex-marriage/upgBZbZ9IvJXY0ZMOElgtN/story.html
35. "US women working percentage stagnant while others grow," http://www.eoionline.org/blog/us-women-working-percentage-stagnant-while-others-grow/
36. "The strange case of the missing baby," http://www.economist.com/news/international/21697817-financial-crisis-hit-birth-rates-fell-rich-countries-expected
37. Hanna Rosin, "The End of Men," http://www.theatlantic.com/magazine/archive/2010/07/the-end-of-men/308135/
38. "Why young men delay adulthood to stay in "Guyland"," http://www.newsweek.com/why-young-men-delay-adulthood-stay-guyland-87539
39. John G. Paton, *Missionary to the New Hebrides: An Autobiography* (London: Hodder & Stoughton, 1891), 4.
40. Hans Bader, "Obamacare Provides $7,200 'Divorce Incentive,' $11,000 for Older Couples," http://www.cnsnews.com/commentary/hans-bader/obamacare-provides-7200-divorce-incentive-11000-older-couples

41. Emma Brockes, "Why Obama won the women's vote," http://www.theguardian.com/world/2012/nov/07/why-obama-won-womens-vote

42. Allan C. Carlson, *Third Ways: How Bulgarian Greens, Swedish Housewives, and Beer-Swilling Englishmen Created Family-Centered Economies - And Why They Disappeared* (Wilmington: ISI Books, 2007), 176-177.

43. There were 22 million farms in 1880. See "History of agriculture in the United States," http://en.wikipedia.org/wiki/History_of_agriculture_in_the_United_States. This accounts for about 45% of the population (since the population was 50,200,000 per the 1880 census). See "1880 United States Census," http://en.wikipedia.org/wiki/1880_United_States_Census. As of 2008, only 2% were employed in agriculture (see the USDA website), with the national self-employment ratio hovering around 11%. This amounts to about 5 times more corporate servitude (conservatively speaking) than there was 120 years ago. In 1900, there was approximately $1 billion in home mortgages, according to the 1969 Statistical Abstract of the United States. Given that the GDP was $20 billion in 1900, this debt accounts for 5% of the GDP. According to the Federal Reserve Bank, Mortgage Debt in the United States stands at $14 trillion or 95% of the GDP (as of 2010). Compare this to 1900, and the debt-load ratio has increased by a factor of almost twenty times. Government spending at all levels (Federal, State, and Local) in 2010 added up to about $7.3 Trillion (including $1.3 Trillion in the Federal Deficit). This accounts for 52.1% of the GDP. In 1900, government spending stood at $1.608 billion or 8% of the GDP. This represents an increase in government tyranny of 6.5 fold since 1900. Moreover, there are 30 times more government regulations (as determined by pages of Federal Register) now than there was in 1936.

44. Magali Rheault, "Most Americans Don't Expect to Receive an Inheritance," http://www.gallup.com/poll/28519/most-americans-dont-expect-receive-inheritance.aspx

45. Tyler Durden, "Baby Boomers Are Drowning In Loans: Debt Of Average 67-Year-Old Soared 169% In Past 12 Years," http://www.zerohedge.com/news/2016-02-12/baby-boomers-are-drowning-loans-debt-average-67-year-old-soared-169-past-12-years

46. Susan Carter and Richard Sutch. "Fixing the Facts: Editing of the 1880 U.S. Census of Occupations with Implications for Long-Term Labor Force Trends and the Sociology of Official Statistics," Historical Methods 29 (1996): 5-24. Bureau of Census. Robert Whaples, Wake Forest University, "Child Labor in the United States," Posted 2010.

47. Cora Sherlock, "92% of Babies With Down Syndrome in England Are Killed in Abortions," http://www.lifenews.com/2014/06/10/92-of-babies-with-down-syndrome-in-england-are-killed-in-abortions/

48. "Marx's Kids Starved as Karl Wrote, Failed Home Economics: Books," http://www.bloomberg.com/news/articles/2011-10-10/marx-s-kids-starved-as-karl-wrote-failed-home-economics-books

49. www.populationpyramid.com

50. Joel Stein, "Millennials: The Me Me Me Generation," http://nation.time.com/millennials/

51. Jason DeParle and Sabrina Tavernise, "For Women Under 30, Most Births Occur Outside Marriage," http://www.nytimes.com/2012/02/18/us/for-women-under-30-most-births-occur-outside-marriage.html?_r=0
52. Nicholas Rayfield, "National student loan debt reaches a bonkers $1.2 trillion," http://college.usatoday.com/2015/04/08/national-student-loan-debt-reaches-a-bonkers-1-2-trillion/
53. Sandy Baum, "The Evolution of Student Debt in the U.S.: An Overview," http://www.upjohn.org/stuloanconf/Baum.pdf
54. http://www.usatoday.com/story/money/columnist/brooks/2013/01/28/retire-debt-crisis-retirement-boomers/1840225/
55. "United States of America, 2014," https://populationpyramid.net/united-states-of-america/2014/
56. Todd Campbell, "It Would Be Dumb To Ignore These 5 Social Security Facts," http://www.fool.com/investing/2016/05/27/it-would-be-dumb-to-ignore-these-social-security-f.aspx
57. Tim Henderson, "More Americans living alone, census says," https://www.washingtonpost.com/politics/more-americans-living-alone-census-says/2014/09/28/67e1d02e-473a-11e4-b72e-d60a9229cc10_story.html
58. Oxford English Dictionary Definition.
59. Johnny Cash, *Cash: The Autobiography*, (New York: HarperCollins, 1997), 21. Italics added.
60. www.covenanteyes.com
61. Belinda Luscombe, "Porn and the Threat to Virility," http://time.com/4277510/porn-and-the-threat-to-virility/?iid=toc_033116
62. "Parents Describe How They Raise Their Children," https://www.barna.org/component/content/article/5-barna-update/45-barna-update-sp-657/184-parents-describe-how-they-raise-their-children
63. www.pewresearch.com
64. "Millennials," http://www.pewresearch.org/topics/millennials/
65. My full study of education in Christian history is available in a book called *Keep the Faith: On Education*, available from generations.org.
66. Aristotle, *Ethics*, Book IV.9.
67. Martin Luther, "Letter to John Lang at Erfurt," February 8, 1517.
68. We recommend the Worldviews in Conflict Curriculum available from generations.org for an example of a right interaction with classic literature and the "great" thinkers of the last 300 years.
69. Jillian Berman, "Here's how much student-loan debt has exploded over the past decade," http://www.marketwatch.com/story/the-average-student-loan-debt-grew-56-over-the-past-10-years-2015-10-27
70. Josh Butler, "Global Youth Unemployment Rate Rising Rapidly," http://www.mintpressnews.com/global-youth-unemployment-rate-rising-rapidly/201978/
71. Brad Plumer, "Only 27 percent of college grads have a job related to their major," https://www.washingtonpost.com/news/wonk/wp/2013/05/20/only-27-percent-of-college-grads-have-a-job-related-to-their-major/
72. Daniel Burke, "Millennials leaving church in droves, study finds," http://www.cnn.com/2015/05/12/living/pew-religion-study/

73. "Barna Survey Examines Changes in Worldview Among Christians over the Past 13 Years," https://www.barna.org/barna-update/transformation/252-barna-survey-examines-changes-in-worldview-among-christians-over-the-past-13-years#.V0POh5MrLq0

74. Will and Ariel Durant, *Rousseau and Revolution* (New York: Simon and Schuster, 1967), 179.

75. John Taylor Gatto, *The Underground History of American Education* (Odysseus Group, 2000).

76. Plato, *The Republic*, Book 5, Section 2, Part 6.

77. Plato, *Laws*, 804d.

78. www.christian.org

79. Ibid.

SCRIPTURE INDEX

Genesis
1:27-28 — 31
1:28 — 27
2:18 — 38, 113
2:18-22 — 27
2:20-22 — 28
9:1 — 31

Exodus
12:26-27 — 75
13:8 — 163
13:14 — 75, 163
20:6 — 139
20:7 — 69
20:8-10 — 115
20:12 — 86, 125
20:13 — 34
21:16-20 — 188
21:22 — 188
21:22-24 — 190
21:22-25 — 33
22:16 — 188
22:22-24 — 14

Leviticus
18:7 — 190
18:29 — 190
19:3 — 126
20:11 — 190
20:17 — 190

Numbers
30:1-15 — 188

Deuteronomy
5:10 — 97

5:16 — 139
6:4 — 65
6:7 — 27, 59, 65, 101, 103, 121, 162, 171, 178, 179, 188, 195
6:7-9 — 49, 64, 75, 120, 165
6:20 — 163
6:20-25 — 75
7:9 — 97
11:1 — 97
14:28-29 — 132
16 — 156
16:9-14 — 178
16:11 — 150
28:18 — 36
28:32 — 189
28:44 — 36
32:46 — 178

Joshua
8:34-35 — 178

1 Samuel
2:29 — 68
3:13 — 68
8:11 — 188
8:11-15 — 189
8:13 — 115
8:18 — 188

2 Chronicles
20:13 — 178

Ezra
10:1 — 178

Nehemiah
1:5 — 97
4:14 — 27
8:2 — 178
12:43 — 178

Job
13:15 — 18

Psalm
1:1-3 — 79
8:2 — 180
19:7 — 92
23 — 50
34:11 — 69
40:8 — 128
51:5 — 85
51:17 — 14
89 — 50
112:1-2 — 67, 139
119:97 — 98
127 — 36
128:1-4 — 67

Proverbs
1:1-6 — 77, 159
1:7 — 166, 175
1:8 — 126
2:4 — 159
2:5 — 159
2:9 — 159
4:11 — 159
4:14 — 159
4:18 — 159
4:26 — 159

4:27   159
6:20-22   140
7   75
9:10   126
11:14   8
13:20   144
13:22   119
13:24   91, 101, 103
14:26   68
16:33   100
21:4   170
23:13   92
23:13-14   92
23:14   91
23:17   66
23:26   169
29:15   92
30:17   88
31   121, 123
31:10-12   114
31:11   11
31:27   28

Song of Songs
8:8-12   163

Isaiah
3:12   36
48:22   39
57:21   39

Jeremiah
13:23   85
17:9   85

Ezekiel
16:21   180

Daniel

9:4   97

Joel
2:15-16   178
2:28   44

Malachi
2:15   37, 41, 180
2:15-16   38
4:5-6   44
4:6   82, 135, 137

Matthew
5:3   14
6:33   34
7:1-5   57
7:23   97, 107
10:39   35
10:40   40
13:1-23   103
15:1-6   127, 128
15:1-8   107
15:3-4   87
15:4-6   162
15:5-6   178
15:6   45, 121, 176
15:6-8   98
17:5   173
18:6   185
19:4-6   23
19:5   116
19:5-6   111
19:10-21 22
19:14   178
22:38   18
23:23   96
23:24   96
23:27   93
25:31-46 128

25:40   133
28:18-20 38

Luke
6:40   46
6:45   186
10:25-37 132
13:3   145
13:5   145
18:13   14, 15

John
3:21   7
4:34   128
6:63   73
6:66-68   73
14:6   173
14:7-9   68
14:15   90, 97
15:13   170
17   69
19   128

Acts
2   64, 178
2:40   75
2:41-47   48
15   178
16:31   60
16:31-34 16
20:7-12   178

Romans
1:24   36
1:26-28   13
3:10-12   85
3:19   90
7:1-4   90
7:7   90, 90

7:22	98
8:9	60
8:28	18
10:14-15	181, 192
12:9	52, 57
12:19	28
13:1	190
13:3-4	90
13:4	28
13:8-9	90
13:8-10	54
14	156
14:5-8	149
14:23	35
15:7	40

1 Corinthians

1:2	178
1:18-27	181
1:22	161
1:22-23	168
1:24	161
2:6	161
5	183
7:3	27, 28
7:5	34
7:9	21, 23
7:14	37, 178
7:18-19	59
7:25-26	21
8:1	168
11:29	182
12:4-12	163
12:13	182
13	54, 55
13:1-4	57
14:15	148, 154
14:26	153
14:34-35	27

16:15	183

2 Corinthians

2:16	15
5:14	74
6:17	185
10:4-5	191
10:5	148
12:14	119, 135

Galatians

4:3	99
5:19-23	60

Ephesians

1:3	68
2:8-9	15, 90
2:14	39
4:11	77
4:14	76
4:26	61
4:32	50, 63
5:18-20	48
5:22	28
5:22-33	29, 30
5:23	24, 28
5:25	27
5:32	24
6:1	29, 39
6:1-4	162, 178, 192
6:2-3	125
6:4	27, 37, 43, 47, 73, 75, 178, 179, 188, 195

Philippians

2:4	128
2:11-12	15
4:8	153

Colossians

1:17	172
2:8	99, 161
2:21	99
3:1-4	69
3:16	148, 155
3:16-17	48, 70
3:18	29, 39
3:20	178
3:20-21	162

1 Thessalonians

2:11	162, 188
5:14	75
5:16	49
5:17	79
5:19-20	183

2 Thessalonians

3:10-15	129
3:14	75

1 Timothy

1:9-10	90
2:9	93
3:1-8	183
4:1-3	21
5	136
5:8	11, 27, 129
5:14	11, 28
5:14-15	21, 23

2 Timothy

3:5	93

Titus

2	146
2:4	28, 121, 159

2:5   28
2:6   159
2:7   159

Hebrews
1:3   173
3:13   39, 71, 73, 74, 82
10:25   74
11:6   16, 67
12:6-8   91
12:25-26   173
13:1-3   185, 192

James
1:22-24   168, 175
1:27   133
2:24   107
2:26   90
4:4   39
4:6   107
5:16   35

1 Peter
2:15-3:4   30
3:4   93
3:7   27
3:15   171
5:5-6   62

2 Peter
1:10   52

1 John
1:8-9   183
2:6   128
2:17   191
3:22   90
4:7-15   183

4:10-12   55
5:3   97

2 John
1:6   97

3 John
1:4   20, 61, 194

Revelation
3:17   14